WHAT PARENTS HAVE SAID ABOUT SENG GROUPS

- *"The class and book have been a life saver! I can't say enough good about them and feel that every parent should have the opportunity to be in a SENG group!"*

- *"I came into this class a little nervous and wondering what I would learn, just like everyone else. I'm leaving it knowing that I have made some good friendships and have gained a lot of knowledge about myself, my child, and how he perceives the world."*

- *"I began this class because I wanted to improve my relationship with my daughter and understand the traits of a gifted child. I thought I was taking the class for her, but discovered that I'm really taking if for myself and feel that I've learned an immense amount about why I am the way I am."*

- *"After my child's attempted suicide, we have been able to re-establish self-esteem for the child and for the family."*

- *"The attitude at school is completely different this year. The principal and several teachers have made special efforts and have remarked upon the change in my son. Twenty-eight discipline slips last year at this time!"*

- *"I strongly recommend the SENG groups! Gifted children are demanding—time as well as energy. This type of class helps to diffuse parental stress as well as present new ideas and techniques."*

- *"Our child has said, 'I feel good that you're going to the trouble to take this class.'"*

- *"I discovered that I am a tradition breaker and was perhaps a gifted child. That makes me feel better about myself and gives me a positive self-image."*

- *"There is not enough space to say all of the POSITIVE things that have come out of this program. This has been ten weeks of positive reinforcement ending in a closer family, a happier, more well-adjusted student, and a more relaxed and secure parent."*

- *"My child's a happier child, my family a healthier family, and I'm a better person as a result of the group. Thank you!"*

"Flowing with rather than fighting against"

GIFTED PARENT GROUPS: THE SENG MODEL

James T. Webb, Ph.D.
Arlene R. DeVries, M.S.E.

Gifted Psychology Press, Inc.
1998

Cover Design: Jacob Lewis
Interior Design: Spring Winnette
Copy Editor: Jennifer Ault

Published by **Gifted Psychology Press, Inc.** (Formerly Ohio Psychology Press)
P.O. Box 5057
Scottsdale, AZ 85261
www.GiftedPsychologyPress.com

Printed and bound in the United States of America.
03 02 01 00 99 98   6 5 4 3 2 1

Library of Congress Cataloguing-in-Publication Data

Webb, James T.
    Gifted Parent Groups: The SENG Model / James T. Webb and Arlene R. DeVries.
            p   .cm.
    Includes bibliographical references and index
    ISBN 0-910701-29-4
    1. Parents of gifted children—Counseling of. 2. Gifted children—Care—Study and teaching
    3. Group counseling of parents — Handbooks, manuals, etc. I. DeVries, Arlene, 1941- .
II. Title.
HQ773.5.W4 1998   98-21448
649'.155—dc21   CIP
ISBN: 0-910701-29-4

Acknowledgments

In 1981, the SENG (Supporting Emotional Needs of Gifted) program began guided discussion groups for parents of able, bright, creative youngsters. Betty Meckstroth, M.S.W., a parent of two gifted children, contributed very much in the early stages and helped to develop both the format and content of these groups. Her valuable contributions have benefitted many parents—both then and now.

With each session, we learned from the parents who attended, and we continue to learn from them today. These dedicated and caring parents not only have helped us understand the diverse challenges and joys of raising talented children, but also have often given of their time to help us teach other facilitators so that they, too, might establish similarly successful guided discussion groups in their communities. To all of these parents, we are extremely grateful.

We also wish to thank Glen Alsop of the Melbourne, Australia CHIP (Children of High Intellectual Potential) Foundation. Her tenure as a visiting scholar at SENG in 1991-1992 provided the impetus to translate our knowledge into this manual. Spring Winnette and Jennifer Ault, our design and copy editors, were key in making this book so readable. We are indebted to them for their care and precision.

To these people, and to many others who have influenced and helped us, our heartfelt thanks. You have made a difference in the lives of many others.

James T. Webb, Ph.D.
Arlene R. DeVries, M.S.E.

Table of Contents

Page

TABLES

Introduction

In our work in the field of gifted and talented, we have often said that parents are our most favorite group to talk to and to work with. Parents of gifted children are so very important, but yet they often lack access to information about the characteristics, behaviors, problems and resources for gifted children. The SENG (Supporting Emotional Needs of Gifted) model for parent groups, which is described in this book, helps to meet some of the needs of parents of gifted children.

This training manual, *Gifted Parent Groups: The SENG Model*, is intended to assist in training facilitators to establish specific guided discussion groups for parents of talented youngsters. These groups help parents better understand, encourage and nurture their gifted children to develop positive self-esteem and enhanced interpersonal skills. The SENG model that we have developed is very describable and is predictable in its implementation, as has been demonstrated over many years of use.

Ordinarily, this training manual is used to accompany a two day workshop to train facilitators in this SENG model of parent guided discussion groups. The two day workshop includes information about setting up the groups, weekly discussion topics, group dynamics, demonstrations, handouts, role-plays of parent groups and specific information about referrals, fees, materials, etc. Most importantly, the two-day training workshop gives trainees an opportunity to actually facilitate a parent group using the SENG model, while simultaneously receiving support, guidance and advice from the trainers. Our experience over the last several years strongly demonstrates that participation in such an organized workshop format for the training is most desirable. These SENG parent group workshops can be arranged by contacting either author directly using the information listed in the *About the Authors* section of this book.

Sometimes, however, it is not feasible for a person to participate in the two day training workshop. In these cases, this training manual may be used alone, though with suitable caution. We would strongly encourage you to consult with others who have already led SENG groups. There is no substitute for experience!

As discussed more fully later, facilitators of the SENG model guided discussion groups need not be trained mental health professionals. These groups are not therapy groups, and facilitators do not need the high level of professional training in group dynamics that otherwise might be expected. Facilitators successfully trained in past workshops include teachers, guidance counselors, coordinators of gifted programs, school psychologists, social workers and parents from the community. A facilitator can be any individual with experience in parenting or teaching gifted children who has also had some experience in group interactions.

The SENG model is structured around bringing together interested parents of talented children in a small group to discuss such topics as motivation, discipline, stress management and peer relationships. What is recognized by the SENG parent group process is that, given a non-judgmental and nurturing atmosphere, the parents of high ability children are themselves a rich resource of information. These groups are co-facilitated by persons with knowledge about parenting and about educating gifted/talented children. The groups meet regularly for a set number of weeks—usually ten weeks. Since the SENG group model does require co-facilitators (i.e., two or three co-leaders) for the parent groups, it is recommended that two or three persons from the same locale receive the training described in this manual prior to starting parent groups. In this way, they will be able to work together better. Prior to the training, it is also strongly recommended that two books be read: *Guiding the Gifted Child: A Practical Source for Parents and Teachers* (Webb, Meckstroth and Tolan, 1982) and *Children: The Challenge* (Dreikurs and Soltz, 1964). Many of the specific techniques and approaches referred to in this training manual are more fully described in these two books. Use of this training manual—and learning to become a facilitator of SENG parent support groups—will be far easier and smoother after digesting the information from these sources.

After completing the two day training (which includes role-plays and practice at facilitating the groups), the trainees should be ready to implement a ten session guided discussion group series within their community using the SENG model. An *Action Plan* and a *Planning Checklist* to assist in implementing specific steps are included in this training manual to help in establishing SENG model parent groups. Throughout this training manual, we have reproduced sample letters and forms that can be copied for use as they are or which may be modified to suit local needs. Likewise, we have included *Appendices* which list additional resources and which contain a great deal of useful information for parents and teachers of gifted and talented children.

You will note some repetition as you read this book. We have done this purposefully for emphasis. In general, we have introduced concepts early to provide an overall framework and then later have re-introduced the concepts to discuss them more fully. We hope you do not find the redundancy to be excessive.

We appreciate your interest in establishing SENG model support groups for parents of gifted children. These parents need and deserve our support as they learn to guide their talented youngsters. We believe that you will find these groups to be as exciting and rewarding as we have.

Jim Webb
Arlene DeVries

CHAPTER I
Background of the SENG Groups

"Children begin by loving their parents; as they grow older they judge them; sometimes they forgive them."
–Oscar Wilde

"Since when was genius found respectable?"
–Elizabeth Barrett Browning

"For precocity, some great price is always demanded sooner or later in life."
–Margaret Ossoli

WHY GUIDED PARENT DISCUSSION GROUPS ARE NEEDED

Parents are a child's first teacher, and parents continue to be teachers throughout the child's life. To be effective teachers and support advocates, however, parents themselves continually need sources of information and support. Parents of gifted children can find such resources through SENG guided discussion groups.

As will be described subsequently, several predictions can be made about parents of talented children. One prediction is that these parents have experienced extremely few settings where they can talk about their children's development and their parenting experiences. Often, they cannot even talk freely with family or friends about their specific child-rearing experiences and issues. Another prediction is that these parents have found very few professionals, including those in schools, with information that is specifically focused on parenting talented and gifted children or who are willing to spare the time for the lengthy discussions involved. As a result, parents of gifted children—particularly highly gifted—often desperately want to discuss their experiences but feel frustrated, pent-up, and alone in their situations.

Parents of high potential children relate repeatedly that they have been unable to share family experiences with other parents whose children are less able. Indeed, parents of average ability children often do have difficulty understanding, relating to, or even believing the parenting experiences which may be told by parents of talented children. After all, it is not unusual for gifted children that a three year old could be reading or that a four year old needs only six hours of sleep. As a result, most parents of bright children quickly learn to downplay or disguise their children's behaviors, and their conversations with other parents are hesitant ones. These parents also often worry that their children are "abnormal," since they lack information that indicates that the behaviors which their gifted children are showing are usually typical of bright, high potential children. Such common gifted child characteristics as imaginary playmates, bossiness, intense dreams and nightmares, or unusual tactile or emotional sensitivities are particularly likely to cause worry for parents.

Often, parents are puzzled by behaviors arising from their children's extreme curiosity, intensity and sensitivity (which characterize children of enhanced learning potential) since these behaviors seem strange and out of place as compared to other children. Preschool children who demonstrate an insatiable and exhausting curiosity or who seem driven to organize and categorize can be quite stressful to parents. As a group, then, parents of children with high intellectual abilities frequently feel isolated from the normal support networks: family, friends, neighbors. Even pediatricians seldom offer more information than, "You sure have a bright child there!"

Parents of gifted children experience an unsettling dissonance between the child-rearing practices recommended for an average child and the reality of the child in their midst. As Seagoe (1974) pointed out, the very strengths and characteristics of talented children often result in associated problems, particularly in social and emotional areas. An adaptation of Seagoe's list is shown in Table 1.

TABLE 1. *Strengths and Problems of Gifted Children*	
Strengths	*Possible Problems*
• Acquires and retains information quickly.	• Impatient with slowness of others; dislikes routine and drill; may resist mastering foundation skills; may make concepts unduly complex.
• Inquisitive attitude; intellectual curiosity; intrinsic motivation; searches for significance.	• Asks embarrassing questions; strong-willed; resists direction; seems excessive in interests; expects same of others.
• Ability to conceptualize, abstract, synthesize; enjoys problem solving and intellectual activity.	• Rejects or omits details; resists practice or drill; questions teaching procedures.
• Can see cause-effect relations.	• Difficulty accepting the illogical, such as feelings, traditions, or matters to be taken on faith.
• Love of truth, equity and fair play.	• Difficulty in being practical; worry about humanitarian concerns.
• Enjoys organizing things and people into structure and order; seeks to systematize.	• Constructs complicated rules or systems; may be seen as bossy, rude, or domineering.
• Large vocabulary and facile verbal proficiency; broad information in advanced areas.	• May use words to escape or avoid situations; becomes bored with school and age-peers; seen by others as a "know it all."

TABLE 1. *Strengths and Problems of Gifted Children* (cont'd)

Strengths	Possible Problems
• Thinks critically; has high expectancies; is self-critical and evaluates others.	• Critical or intolerant toward others; may bcome discouraged or depressed; perfectionistic.
• Keen observer; willing to consider the unusual; open to new experiences.	• Overly intense focus; occasional gullibility.
• Creative and inventive; likes new ways of doing things.	• May disrupt plans or reject what is already known; seen by others as different and out of step.
• Intense concentration; long attention span in areas of interest; goal directed behavior; persistence.	• Resists interruption; neglects duties or people during periods of focused interests; stubbornness.
• Sensitivity; empathy for others; desire to be accepted by others.	• Sensitivity to criticism or peer rejection; expects others to have similar values; need for success and recognition; may feel different and alienated.
• High energy, alertness, eagerness; periods of intense efforts.	• Frustration with inactivity; eagerness may disrupt others' schedules; needs continual stimulation; may be seen as hyperactive.
• Independent; prefers individualized work; self-reliant.	• May reject parent or peer input; non-conformity; may be unconventional.
• Diverse interests and abilities; versatility.	• May appear scattered and disorganized; frustrations over lack of time; others may expect continual competence.
• Strong sense of humor.	• Sees absurdities of situations; humor may not be understood by peers; may become "class clown" to gain attention.

Because of the lack of information about characteristics of gifted children, a substantial number of parents will be unsure if their child is indeed talented, gifted, or otherwise intellectually unusual. Some parents are under the misapprehension that all gifted children are geniuses. Yet other parents cannot see how their child could possibly be gifted, since the child's judgment lags so far behind his intellect. ("For someone so bright, he has no common sense at all!") Even after a child has been formally identified as "gifted," the parents—most often the father—may remain uncertain or doubtful, as though their child really might be an impostor who has fooled the professionals at school

Because of this, parents of children with high intellectual potential have a particular need to communicate with other parents of gifted children in order to share their similar parenting experiences in an understanding manner. It is equally important for these parents to receive information and guidance about gifted children and their characteristics in ways which will allow them to provide parenting which will enhance—not thwart—the intellectual and emotional development of their children's potentials.

In short, these parents need resources, along with a special place where they can consider these resources and be encouraged to apply them within their families. The SENG model guided discussion group for parents provides exactly such opportunities for these parents. The objectives of the SENG parent support groups, which stem directly from these needs, are summarized in Table 2.

TABLE 2. *Objectives of SENG Model Parent Support Groups*

1. Increase parents' awareness that talented children and their families have special emotional needs.

2. Enhance parenting skills for nurturing emotional development of talented children and their families.

3. Provide parents with materials to promote understanding of:

    a. characteristics of high potential children;

    b. programs and opportunities for talented children;

    c. books and professional organizations in the field of the talented;

    d. referrals for more in-depth professional assistance.

TABLE 2. *Objectives of SENG Model Parent Support Groups* *(cont'd)*
4. Establish an environment where parents of talented children can interact with other parents and with facilitators who will provide support, guidance and professional advice.
5. Encourage appropriate parent involvement with and support of educational opportunities.

Since 1981, numerous guided discussion groups for parents of high potential/gifted children have been conducted using this SENG model, and refinements have been made in the ensuing years. From the very beginning, these parent groups were found to have clear and predictable patterns, and the role of the facilitators was one that could be described. Similarly, a variety of specific identifiable facilitator techniques were noted as being extremely helpful within these groups. It also became apparent that the SENG model is one that can be implemented in many locations with a wide range of parents. As a result, training workshops have been conducted over the past 15 years in many states, as well as outside of the United States, and as of 1998, over 350 facilitators in 15 states have been trained. SENG parent groups are being conducted in English, Spanish, Russian, Hmong and Urdu, perhaps in other languages as well, and the SENG model appears effective in all. Reports from these facilitators and from parents continue to affirm the validity of the model and the importance of these groups, not only in terms of enhancing effective parenting, but also in promoting better relations between parents and school personnel regarding talented children.

HISTORICAL PERSPECTIVE AND OVERVIEW

In 1980, an extremely bright 16 year old from Dayton, Ohio, committed suicide. Even prior to his death, his parents, who had obtained professional help for this young man, had become aware of how scarce the resources were for families of such intellectually high potential youngsters, particularly to help with social and emotional needs. Although many programs existed nationwide to provide academic enrichment, they found that psychological support systems focusing on social and emotional issues (such as self-esteem, peer relations and family relationships) were essentially non-existent. As a result, Dr. and Mrs. Egbert, the parents of this youngster, asked the School of Professional Psychology at Wright State University to initiate such a program for families with gifted children. In January, 1981, *The Phil Donahue Show* focused on the topic of gifted children, depression and suicide. Subsequently, more than 20,000 letters were sent to this national TV show and to the National Association for Gifted Children confirming, sadly enough, that there was a widespread need to provide resources and services for parents of gifted children, and that extremely few support services were available. It was from this background that the SENG (Supporting Emotional Needs of Gifted) program was born, and it continues into the present to hold annual national conferences and to provide other services for parents and teachers concerning the social and emotional needs of gifted children. (The SENG program now is headquartered at Kent State University, P.O. Box 5190, Kent, OH 44242.)

From the outset, SENG has emphasized working with parents because of the belief in their importance in the lives of the children. The guided discussion groups were established as a setting where parents could share information and concerns. It was decided that the groups would meet once each week for one and one half hours, and ten topics were selected for discussion. Each of these ten weekly sessions emphasize one topic of importance concerning social and emotional needs. These weekly topics, in the order in which they are considered in the SENG parent support groups, are:

1. Identification
2. Motivation
3. Discipline
4. Stress Management
5. Depression

6. Communication of Feelings
7. Peer Relationships
8. Sibling Relationships
9. Tradition Breaking
10. Parent Relationships

These ten topics were selected because they are frequent problem areas encountered specifically by gifted children, their siblings and their parents. The sequence was chosen because it is one that flows naturally from one topic to the next. In each session, parents share information, situations, common experiences and concerns. The group facilitators and other parents offer comments, advice and guidance. To insure that the groups are more than just "gripe groups" or "coffee Klatches," the facilitators encourage parents at the end of each session to reflect on what ideas or suggestions have specific "take home" value for them. The parents are then encouraged to implement these suggestions within their families, with their children, or with the school and to bring back their results to the group the following week.

The parent group sessions are held one week apart. Although some persons have suggested meeting more frequently, our experience shows that an entire week is needed between topics so that participants can absorb and implement the information shared into their own families and to observe its effects. Some persons also have suggested meeting for only six or seven weeks, since ten weeks represents such a significant time commitment. Again, our experience has been that each of the ten topics warrants a separate focus and that ten weeks is needed for parents to try their "homework," to make needed adjustments and to see the results within the family.

Parents who sign up for the group are provided reading material prior to attending the meetings. During the first two years of the development of SENG, the group leaders provided handouts on each of the above ten topics. Over time, the handouts grew—often from information learned from parents in the groups—and resulted in the book *Guiding the Gifted Child* (Webb, Meckstroth and Tolan, 1982), which has sold over 100,000 copies. Subsequently, this book has become the basic framework around which these parent groups are organized, and each family is provided with a copy prior to the first session. Even so, additional material is often brought in by the group leaders or sometimes by the parents themselves. *ERIC Digest* articles, reprints from the National Center for Research on Gifted and Talented, or other handouts can be particularly useful in focusing on recent trends or research findings.

It is important to emphasize that the SENG groups are *not* therapy groups. Likewise, they are *not* advocacy groups, although advocacy efforts are worthwhile, and other advocacy groups may be encouraged in different settings. Rather, they are guidance groups concerned with the prevention of problems and with handling child-rearing and other similar life situations that pose concerns or which possibly could get out of hand.

The groups provide a forum for parents of gifted children to gain exposure to a variety of parent-child experiences, to "swap parenting recipes" and to gain insight into how their parenting styles can prevent or ameliorate (or sometimes cause) problems. The groups are based on an assumption that the best way to solve problems is to prevent them, and they try to build problem-solving techniques to help correct difficulties that are likely to arise.

A further assumption, however, is that "there are two types of people in this world—those who have problems, and those you don't know well enough yet to know that they have problems." We don't wish to appear naive. Certainly, life has problems and the SENG groups discuss them, but the focus continues to be on methods for encouraging positive growth that can prevent behavioral and emotional problems. Where problems exist, group members are encouraged to use them as opportunities for growth rather than as triggers for blame. Often, it is possible for a person to use a potential problem in a healthy, growth-oriented fashion rather than to passively accentuate its negative consequences.

Of course, some family or personal problems are larger than others. If these situations are already causing serious problems, parents are encouraged to see professionals outside of the SENG groups for individual help, usually in addition to attending the group sessions. It is desirable, then, that the facilitators have knowledge of at least one or two mental health professionals or other resources to whom referrals might be made should the necessity arise. This is not meant to imply that facilitators should incur a legal risk through such a referral. Part of the facilitator training includes discussing how one can encourage seeking outside help without inappropriately endorsing a psychologist, physician, counselor, or agency.

Appropriate advocacy in the gifted child field is certainly needed. Thus, it also helps for facilitators to know of advocacy groups so that parents might be referred to them. Organized advocacy efforts are needed with schools, courts, legislators, etc., on behalf of gifted children (Karnes and Marquardt, 1991a; 1991b) if gifted children are to obtain needed recognition and support. Advocacy groups do provide one kind of support for parents; however, the SENG guided discussion groups, as noted previously, are not designed to be advocacy groups. The facilitators, then, will steer parent advocacy efforts elsewhere beyond the SENG groups.

During its development, the SENG model guided support groups for parents emerged as a model that was effective and could be exported through training to other locations. Additionally, because the model is aimed at parenting rather than advocacy, it is not threatening to school systems or administrations and hopefully can be supported by them. Since it seeks to empower parents to support and protect the emotional growth of their children, the

SENG model is actually likely to reduce the intensity of confrontations between parents and education systems.

The success of the groups has been eloquent testimony to their effectiveness. What parents primarily learn is that they have it within themselves to guide and nurture their own children. At the same time, it has been the experience of the SENG program that parents in the groups often come to a better understanding of themselves, perhaps their own giftedness. Specifically, parents often learn ways to avoid becoming engaged in power struggles, learn better ways of enhancing motivation and are able to apply many techniques and approaches which enhance communication and deepen their relationships with their children. Perhaps most of all, the SENG model parent groups preserve a sense of optimism and focus on the importance of the family.

We hope that the following sections will provide the information needed to establish similar SENG model parent groups within your community. The techniques and approaches described in this SENG model are not held out as being the *only* workable model with parents of talented children. However, the SENG model is clearly one successful model that has proven itself. The advice and recommendations contained within this training manual will help you to profit from our experiences about behaviors that seem to work for facilitators, as well as those behaviors to be avoided.

What SENG Parent Groups Are (and are not)

SENG parent groups are guided discussion groups. They are highly supportive of their participants. The dynamics within the group encourage a sharing of parenting ideas which, through the facilitated discussion, allows the parents to select those alternatives which seem most relevant and useful within their families for their talented children.

The role of the facilitators is *not* one of lecturing, teaching, or even of being the person of authority; instead, the facilitators primarily draw upon the experiences of the parents themselves. Said in a different fashion, the co-facilitators take the role of "the guide from the side," rather than "the sage from the stage." Through gentle questioning, occasionally providing information and modeling positive techniques, the facilitators create a group climate which provides a safe environment for parents to share not only their successes, but also their concerns and difficulties. Such an environment allows the opportunity for parents to question the assumptions underlying their current parenting practices and then to try alternative, new and generally less confrontational parenting approaches. Throughout the group discussions, the facilitators reinforce and underscore the positive steps while simultaneously weaving into the discussions various key concepts.

Certainly, the groups also provide information. This information comes primarily from information already possessed by the parents who attend, but also from books, handouts, journals and articles which promote the understanding of affective and cognitive characteristics of gifted and talented children. Thus, the group itself is able to act as an informational resource while still allowing the group facilitators to add more information and foster insights, yet avoid being viewed as "the expert who knows the *right* way to parent gifted children."

A basic assumption of the SENG parent groups (which has emerged through experience) is that parents of high ability children are, themselves, a tremendously rich resource of information—at least about their own children and family experiences—and are willing to share that information when given a non-judgmental and nurturing atmosphere. Simultaneously, however, the parents are frequently troubled by self-doubts as they perceive their own shortcomings in relation to the responsibility of raising such a bright child, even though their commitment to their parenting role is clearly present. (A predictable characteristic of these parents is that they are intense and idealistic in the same way that their creative, high potential children are intense and idealistic.)

Several fundamental and basic assumptions underlie the SENG group model and are recurrent themes that the facilitators emphasize repeatedly. Though these key principles are not unique to SENG parent groups, they are nonetheless essential as the foundation upon which these groups operate. These cardinal principles are as follows:

1. It is important to enhance the self-esteem of the child and of the parent. When one is a minority—as gifted children usually are— the ability to believe in oneself becomes particularly important.

2. A healthy, nurturing relationship with the child is of critical importance. If there is at least one relationship in which the child

feels accepted as a person—not just as an achiever—the long-term outcome of the child is likely to be good.

3. The child and parent need to develop a belief-value-ethics philosophy or view of life which incorporates respect and compassion for others and which gives purpose to life.

It is also important to reiterate what SENG groups are not. They are not didactic teaching groups, nor therapy groups, nor advocacy groups. Certainly, such other groups are important, and there is nothing to prevent the parents from participating simultaneously in such other activities elsewhere. However, we have found that the guided discussion groups are most likely to result in significant parental and family growth if the principles and techniques described subsequently are followed by the group facilitators.

GROUP LEADERS:
NECESSARY ATTRIBUTES

What about the facilitators? Can anyone become a facilitator? Our experience is that, although a wide range of people are able to successfully become facilitators, some people are nevertheless more likely than others to become particularly adept and helpful as facilitators. Some of the attributes needed to be a successful facilitator involve having a particular knowledge base; other attributes are personal ones of style of interaction.

It may be a relief to know that one person need not possess all of the necessary relevant information. For optimum effect, SENG parent groups require two (or perhaps three) facilitators in order to satisfactorily monitor and nurture the group process. Not only is the presence of a back-up leader helpful in case one facilitator should become ill, but also having a co-facilitator means that one person can have information that the other does not. Between the two facilitators, a great deal of knowledge and skill is thus present.

Ideally, at least one of the group facilitators should have solid information regarding the special needs and characteristics of children with high intellectual potential. This would include a good working knowledge of social and emotional development, school-based provisions and programming, identification procedures and current research. The other leader certainly could be much less sophisticated in the content area of talented children but should have a substantial amount of experience with regard to parenting, group dynamics, support groups, or interaction skills. Of course, this information can be learned, and we are not implying that one must be an expert from the outset. The references at the end of this manual can be of significant help in these areas.

Of the highest importance is that *all* facilitators have the ability to be patient and non-judgmental. Nothing can ruin a group faster than facilitators impatiently and angrily trying to push parents, teachers, or school systems in their direction. We have heard of some novice facilitators who tried to *demand* that a school system immediately support their efforts to start a group; needless to say, it did *not* work! Likewise, we must emphasize that persons should not become facilitators of these groups to work their own issues or to attack schools. Certainly, the facilitators may often be facing their own personal or parenting issues. Even so, the focus of the facilitators is on conducting the groups, not on favorite issues.

Because many of the facilitators' efforts are toward conducting or guiding the flow of content, it is important that the leaders have good personal rapport with each other. If the leaders are at cross-purposes, the groups will not work. An important maxim in selecting a co-facilitator is to know that person fairly well and to feel comfortable enough to be able to discuss openly what you are doing together. A dogmatic personality who is adamantly committed to a particular viewpoint of parenting or of education would be a high risk for the warm, supportive, explorative nature that is necessary to be a successful group leader. An especially talkative person who facilitates may have difficulty simply guiding or allowing the discourse of others.

The roles of the facilitators outside of the SENG group warrant consideration also. Group leadership by two teachers from the same school district might be inadvisable, as it could set them up as too readily identifiable with that district's particular educational system and philosophy; thus, they might feel that they have to defend it, rather than help parents to understand and explore the school's policies and procedures.

Co-facilitators may wish to consider how they might complement each other through their dress, their personality, and their own parenting experiences. One leader might dress consistently in business suits; the other more casually. Thereby, they reflect differences in style among the parents and encourage a broader atmosphere of acceptance. Similarly, a co-leader with children under ten years of age would share a different range of experiences than the facilitator who has children in late adolescence.

Within these guidelines, we have found that a wide range of persons are successfully able to be quite effective group facilitators. With practice, many persons are able to develop the array of skills necessary to become a successful group facilitator. A successful facilitator need not even be a parent (though the experience of parenthood does provide a certain amount of empathy for other parents). Non-parent facilitators usually need only indicate to the group that they are eager to share information learned from other experiences with talented children, from other parents and from professional literature.

The most important attributes of facilitators are sensitivity, caring about others and the ability to nurture, support and guide parents as they struggle to find answers regarding parenting and educating their complex children. The groups are support groups to share information which is relevant to a variety of parents who have children with a broad range of talents and personalities.

CHAPTER II
About the Parents

"I'd say he's gifted! His mother has tried to give him away several times."

–Jean Watts, *In Search of Perspective*

"That isn't a kid. He's a two-legged stress test!"
–Dennis, The Menace

"Children today are tyrants. They contradict their parents, gobble their food, and tyrannize their teachers."
–Socrates

Facilitators are best able to conduct SENG guided discussion parent groups if they know some of the predictable characteristics that parents of bright children exhibit when they are in these groups. In addition, it helps to know how these characteristics change over the ten session series. Such knowledge helps the facilitator to trust the process, which in turn, helps them to be more comfortable in their facilitating.

CHARACTERISTICS OF PARENTS AT THE FIRST SESSION

Parents of highly able children in SENG guided discussion groups are predictable with regard to their concerns, and the behaviors of the SENG groups show typical patterns. Several characteristics which typify parents at the first session of the SENG parent support groups are summarized in Table 3. These behaviors appear to be characteristic of parents of gifted children in different sections of the country, in rural and urban settings, in various ethnic groups and from diverse socioeconomic levels. Indeed, we have found that these characteristics seem present in parents from other countries as well. The challenges and issues which gifted children pose for their parents are remarkably similar and are a fundamental aspect which underlies the SENG parent support groups.

TABLE 3. *Characteristics of Parents at the First Session*

- Have many questions about gifted/talented children.
- Are highly verbal.
- Possess a great deal of useful information to share.
- Are intense (like their own gifted children).
- Have had few opportunities to share parenting experiences.
- Have many questions about parenting and schooling.
- Feel frustrated with school systems (often angry).
- Form a cohesive group extremely quickly.
- Support and learn from each other.
- Have a good sense of humor.
- Want as much information as possible and want to implement many new ideas.
- Are able to attempt only one to three behavioral changes per week.

As noted previously, the parents bring to the groups a great deal of information about parenting, human behavior and resources for gifted children. However, they also bring to the groups many questions, fears, misconceptions, anxieties and doubts, as well as their own parenting styles which, most often, they learned from their own parents. A conscientious group, these parents are concerned about their own lack of information regarding the implications intellectual giftedness might have on the development of their youngsters. They feel a strong sense of parenting responsibility, but generally believe that their personal knowledge base about parenting their particular child is slim.

Parents bring to the group their insecurities about the characteristics and identification of talented children. As mentioned previously, parents (particularly fathers) are often unsure if indeed their children are gifted. Thus, they bring to the initial session a hesitancy and sometimes an almost apologetic search for information and reassurance. Yet other parents have the notion that all gifted children are like their own child and have not yet experienced the varieties of giftedness. The SENG group experience is one that quickly offers reassurance and enables parents to confront their doubts and seek out the appropriate information about their children's potentials.

Several other characteristics are likewise typical. These parents tend to be intense and highly verbal but have felt isolated in their parenting experiences. As a result, they will form a cohesive group almost instantaneously. "This is the first time I have been able to talk openly about my child," is a statement heard frequently in the first session. Their unmet needs, combined with their intensity, cause the groups to coalesce so firmly that it is often difficult to end the group sessions.

Despite their lack of formal knowledge about identification processes and characteristics of gifted children and despite the frustrations they often have experienced with their children, these parents do, as noted previously, possess a wealth of information. After all, they live with their offspring! Liberating this information is intrinsic to the group process. Most of these parents are very verbal—and if not, are at least very articulate; they generally will exchange information readily.

Because these aspects of the group are so predictable, facilitators are able to assume a role that allows them primarily to highlight, emphasize and underscore appropriate parenting rather than teaching it. Thus, principles and techniques are woven into the fabrics of the lives of the participants, rather than being external, unconnected and artificial to them. This "weave"—

though often seemingly incidental or even casual—is extremely powerful. As will be demonstrated later, the facilitators will try to help parents identify primary threads within their own families and help the parent pull the threads together into a meaningful tapestry of understanding, self-worth and sense of appropriate direction.

It is also common that most parents of high potential children will be frustrated, perhaps angry, with the school experiences their children have received. Indeed, the school system initially tends to be perceived as the source of many difficulties, since so many schools emphasize basic and minimal levels of competence and have few program options for continual progress toward academic excellence.

The exasperation of these parents is understandable. They have children who are exceptional in ability and potential and who have definite educational needs that are exceptions to the schools' usual offerings, but most school systems—particularly public schools—feel that they must focus their efforts primarily on the average or below average child. Although the frustration and anger of the parents may be understandable, these characteristics prompt many school personnel to avoid interacting with them. Administrators often describe these parents as "unguided missiles" who are making special demands for their child and who want exceptions to the system. The result is that school administrators are often reluctant to encourage parents of talented children to organize into groups, while simultaneously, the parents of highly able children progressively feel more isolated.

It is essential that the group facilitators recognize a subsequent typical pattern within the SENG groups. Although the parents initially may be frustrated and angry with the school systems and are often quite vocal about this within the SENG guided discussion groups, it can be predicted that the anger at the school systems will be greatly diluted—often absent—by the end of the third or fourth session. And of course, the facilitators will guide the parents to focus increasingly on family concerns.

Because of the supportive nature of the group and by obtaining more information about talented/gifted/creative children, the parents come to realize that their own interactions with the child (i.e., the family) are far more important in the child's long-term outcome than are schooling experiences. This is not to say that schools are unimportant; far from it! However, parents are the child's first teacher and will continue to be the primary teachers throughout the child's life.

As the group progresses, parents become more accepting of limitations placed on public schools and of the need for parents to help schools rather than simply attack them. They also accept that, as parents, they will themselves likely need to provide enriching experiences for their children. Most of all, the parents become very aware that their relationships with their children and the ways in which they model coping are essential.

Recognition of this shift in attitudes over the first three or four sessions is very important. Otherwise, group facilitators will worry that the group is becoming only a "gripe group." Facilitators can also reassure concerned school administrators that the guided discussion group will not become a frenzied advocacy group. Facilitators, you must trust the process!

This qualitative shift shown by parents during the third or fourth session deserves more comment. Instead of only feeling frustrated and helpless, these parents realize an empowerment from the group. Increasingly, they appreciate that they are able to have a major impact on the development of their children. Although during the first two sessions parents typically want all of the answers immediately (yet another prediction that can be made), the momentum of the group toward mutual problem-solving carries with it a strong sense of shared purpose, optimism and an orientation toward practical application. The thoughtful introspection, patience, support and encouragement (which the facilitators model) helps parents to help their children develop coping skills to deal with life and to function in society.

PREDICTIONS ABOUT PARENTS IN SENG GROUPS

Over fifteen years of experience with SENG groups have revealed some consistent characteristics which the parents show with remarkable predictability. Knowing these predictable behaviors not only prepares group facilitators for what they will encounter in the groups, but also reassures them because of their very predictability. Some of these predictions have been briefly mentioned previously, but deserve specific and separate emphasis.

Prediction One

Parents of high ability children will coalesce into a group extremely quickly. Very seldom have they had the opportunity to talk openly with other parents about their children, yet these parents have intense feelings and a strong need to share.

Prediction Two

Parents of talented children exhibit a profound sense of relief at finding other parents with whom they can talk about their children and their parenting experiences. As noted previously, these parents frequently have encountered disbelief, criticism, or other negative reactions from other parents or family members concerning the characteristics and challenges that they are facing with their children.

Prediction Three

Parents of gifted children show the same high level of intensity which characterizes their children. This intensity will likely manifest itself in virtually all of the feelings and behaviors shown by the parents. When they participate in the group sessions, these parents will participate vigorously. Their feelings about issues will be very keen. Their own lives are typically characterized by strong feelings. This prediction arises out of the observation that most of the parents of gifted children are themselves bright and talented individuals.

Prediction Four

Parents of talented children are highly verbal. In general, the sessions are lively, and group facilitators do not need to say a lot. By the fourth week, the noise level of the group conversations is generally quite loud.

Prediction Five

Parents themselves have a wealth of information which they are eager to share with others. Usually in the first session, but certainly in the second session, most (or probably all) of the parents are eagerly joining in. In fact, it is typically quite difficult to call sessions to a close, and if allowed the opportunity, the group will spontaneously regroup and continue even after the ending time. It is not at all uncommon to discover parents in the parking lot talking animatedly some 30 to 45 minutes later.

Prediction Six

Parents of high ability children have often found that schools have not met their needs, and they often perceive the schools as not being "user-friendly." The parents of such children have approached their schools with many questions and often have asked for educational exceptions to be made for their children. However, most of the parents also have found that administrators of school systems—as they try to cope with overwhelming societal demands—generally try to minimize exceptions. School systems—like other systems—are predicated on trying to handle large groups in the most efficient manner, which in turn, is based on the assumption of basic uniformity of educational experiences. Since talented children often do not fit the school's mold, parents frequently meet resistance when they ask for educational exceptions.

Prediction Seven

Many parents of gifted children will articulate frustration and anger at public schools. In addition to the points made in Prediction Six, parents of gifted children often expect schools to provide optimum experiences for their children, and they have little appreciation that the schools (particularly public schools) are primarily charged with providing a standard education as a first priority. (Nor do parents understand the extent to which our society has required public schools to become "social change agents" for disadvantaged children!)

Facilitators should not be surprised at the anger expressed by the parents, but also must keep in mind that the anger will dissipate for most parents within a short time as they gain more understanding about the role of public education and come to more fully appreciate the great role that parenting has in the long-term outcome of gifted children. Even so, facilitators must take care not to let the groups drift into becoming simply "gripe groups" about schools. Techniques to avoid this will be discussed later.

Prediction Eight

Parents generally want very much to be able to work with schools, despite their disappointments and irritation. By the fourth session of the series, the parents' anger at the schools is usually sharply reduced and, in many cases, virtually non-existent. The parents begin to focus on what they themselves can do. This can provide opportunities for facilitators to encourage more school support and appropriate parent-school relationships.

Prediction Nine

The problems of parenting a gifted child will transcend customary social class or ethnic barriers. The challenges and difficulties involved in parenting a gifted child, as well as the concern for these children by their parents, typically results in parents making friends with (and feeling support from) other parents of similar children, even though their life circumstances may be extremely different from one another. It has been our experience that these friendships often continue well after the groups have ended.

Prediction Ten

Parents are initially impatient for information. End-of-session evaluations from the first three sessions will indicate that the parents want more—they want the answers now. Facilitators must be patient in this regard. Remember, even if you had all the answers, you would not be able to convey all of that information in such a short time, nor would the parents be able to incorporate that much information into their families.

Prediction Eleven

Despite their challenges, the parents exhibit a keen sense of humor and optimism. Their humor becomes a powerful tool. It allows the parents to see the absurdity in many situations as well as to develop or maintain some sense of perspective about themselves and their children.

These groups tend to be fun and are quite stimulating to facilitate. Besides a great deal of laughter, group facilitators typically report that they feel energized by the group.

Prediction Twelve

By the fourth session (sometimes the third), parents begin to report major changes occurring in the family pattern of their interactions with their children. As the parents implement their "homework assignments," they find that positive changes do occur. These reports provide an opportunity for the facilitators to support and reinforce these positive changes to the group as a whole, and a snowballing effect toward positive change begins. Other parents are then heartened and encouraged to pursue their own homework more vigorously, and even further changes result. Often, these changes border on the extraordinary in their effect.

Prediction Thirteen

Although the focus of the group is on the children, the parents characteristically begin to reflect upon themselves—usually by the fourth or fifth session. Comments in the group will reflect that, "these are also issues for ourselves as adults," or "I thought I came here to find out about my child, and I am finding out more about myself." As a result, the parents engage in self-examination, which often changes the way they perceive themselves and the way they interact with others beyond their children.

Prediction Fourteen

By the eighth or ninth session, many parents will have begun talking about wanting to continue the groups beyond the ten weeks allotted. Although this topic routinely arises, it has been our experience that ten weeks is an optimum amount of time. It is difficult for parents to maintain such a weekly commitment beyond ten weeks, particularly if there is not a specific topic of focus each week. If parents want to informally get together, then that is up to them. In fact, some groups have held reunions, usually in conjunction with another information speaker or program.

Prediction Fifteen

During the last five sessions, parents will report an increased frequency of interaction with the schools and that the interactions are more positive. The techniques learned in the group about interacting with their children are also used by these parents in interactions with school personnel. This should be encouraged. Not only has the anger lessened, but the parents are now using (and sometimes labeling) specific techniques from the group sessions in conversations with teachers and school administrators. These techniques, to be described in detail later, include "anticipatory praise," "catching the child doing something right" and "transfer of motivation." Parents report positive results from these interactions.

Prediction Sixteen

Although the groups are not therapy groups, the effects of group participation and the parents' homework will be very therapeutic for the families involved. This is not meant to imply that the parents come into the groups having psychological problems. Some do; most do not. Rather, it implies that, with guidance and a desire to improve, most parents and families could function better, and the experiences within the SENG model support groups help promote such growth.

CHARACTERISTICS OF PARENTS AT THE END OF THE SENG GROUP

At the end of the ten week period, SENG group facilitators can expect to see quite marked changes in the participants. As noted previously, many of the changes are often in the parents' interactions with the school and within themselves, as well as in interactions with their children. Most parents show a dramatically increased sense of perspective and patience with themselves, their children and the school systems. These changes are a function both of the process and the content. It is not simply the gathering together of such parents that produces these striking changes. Instead, it is the entire model: the structuring of the group, the setting where the groups are held, the content that is discussed and the behaviors of the group facilitators. All of these are important elements.

The characteristics of these parents at the end of the SENG groups are summarized in Table 4. Of course, some of these characteristics are the same ones that the parents brought to the group initially, and since they are common to parents of high ability children, will not have changed. These parents remain highly verbal. They are still intense and want the best for their children. They still possess a great deal of knowledge—only now their fund of information is increased and their sense of understanding is expanded. As a result, they have fewer questions to ask about the needs of children of high intellectual potential. Their level of worry and frustration is substantially reduced.

TABLE 4. *Characteristics of Parents at the Last Session*

- Have fewer questions about gifted/talented children.
- Continue to be highly verbal (often more so).
- Possess an increased amount of useful information to share.
- Are intense (like their own gifted children), but have learned better ways of managing their intensity.
- Have fewer questions about parenting and schooling.
- Are less angry at school systems and more focused in their actions.
- Are a cohesive support group; feel less alone.
- Have accomplished major behavioral changes.
- Have a good sense of humor, an increased perspective and more patience.
- Have better relations with their children and with school.
- Have more realistic expectations.

In general, the parents are more optimistic, confident and feel more competent, and they have a sense of perspective that allows them to respond more thoughtfully rather than out of habit or simply out of emotion. The most valuable learning experiences undoubtedly are those relevant to their own parenting styles. They understand themselves and their children much better, and the insights gained and the support they have received enables these parents to better guide the futures of their children.

A substantial number of the parents find that the issues they discuss within the group concerning their children are really continuing issues for themselves as adults. Often, therefore, the parents find that the groups have benefit for them in their adult life in a very therapeutic way, even though these groups are not therapy groups.

Because the parents now have more information and the encouragement and support of the facilitators and other parents in the group, they can become more focused in their own actions. Less angry at school systems and more knowledgeable about the educational needs of high ability children, these parents are in a better position to determine how they might improve conditions for their children and how to support schools in efforts to achieve high quality education. Their advocacy is more reasoned and informed and thus more effective. Though school support is not a direct goal of the SENG parent groups, it is nonetheless a natural and important consequence of the information, support and sense of identity which is derived from the parents' participation in these groups.

Throughout the ten weeks, parents have been encouraged to try alternative behaviors in interacting with their children. With these behavioral changes, the parents establish better relations with their children as well as with the school (especially where reversal in poor school performance has been brought about). Expectations are generally more realistic. Guided and supported by the group and reinforced by the facilitators, the parents have incorporated major changes into the dynamics within their families.

Now that they feel less isolated, these parents can confront the uniqueness of their children. As the group sessions progress, they feel less threatened by the implications of "giftedness." They feel less helpless and have found that there are others who understand and support them. The groups are truly an empowering experience.

CHAPTER III
Specific Content Covered in the Groups

"He who knows others is learned; he who knows himself is wise."
–Lao-Tzsu

"The more intensively the family has stamped its character upon the child, the more it will tend to feel and see its earlier miniature world again in the bigger world of adult life."
–Carl Jung

"The greatest discovery of my generation is that human beings can alter their lives by altering their attitudes of mind."
–William James

We have already noted that it is important for the SENG group facilitators to have reasonable knowledge about the social and emotional characteristics of bright/gifted/talented/high ability children, as well as some information about parenting and interpersonal relations as it relates to enhancing the self-esteem of such youngsters. This does not mean that a facilitator must have all knowledge in this area. Remember, in the land of the blind, one-eyed people are the leaders. It also helps if at least one of the facilitators has some knowledge about educational options for talented children (e.g., enrichment, acceleration, pull-out, cluster grouping, continuous progress, models, etc.). Although the groups focus on parenting, not education, questions about educational approaches do arise, and certainly educational misplacement of gifted children can contribute to social and emotional problems.

Much of the content about the social and emotional needs of gifted children can be found in *Guiding the Gifted Child: A Practical Source for Parents and Teachers* (Webb, Meckstroth and Tolan, 1982), Chapters 3-13. There are other books about gifted children which would be quite helpful, and many of these are listed in the recommended reading list at the end of this manual (*Appendix B—Books for Families with Gifted Children*), as are a variety of books which have proven helpful concerning parenting and self-esteem in general. Of these latter books, *Children: The Challenge* (Dreikurs and Soltz, 1964) has proven itself to be a particularly useful resource. Although that book was not written specifically concerning high ability children, much of its content is highly relevant and practical for talented children. The principles in *Children: The Challenge* help parents avoid getting caught up in power struggles and promote self-management by the child. A large number of highly practical techniques for parents are also described in very readable form.

Primarily, though, the content of the ten sessions in SENG groups is organized around chapters in *Guiding the Gifted Child*. Basically, each chapter forms the foundation for the focus of discussion for one session. Even so, group facilitators may wish to distribute additional materials from other sources (e.g., handouts, copies of articles, etc.). Please note, however, that the group facilitators will weave into the session additional threads from other topics about gifted children (or from other chapters in *Guiding the Gifted Child*) if they seem appropriate to the concerns being discussed at that time by the SENG group. Because this is not a lecture group, it is not necessary to follow a linear style of imparting information. Instead, the style is more conversational, and therefore the content sometimes wanders in the directions that are of concern to the group right then. Of course, the facilitators guide the group back to the focus of the session at a suitable time.

As noted elsewhere, parents are provided a copy of *Guiding the Gifted Child* prior to beginning the parent group series, and they are encouraged to prepare for each session by reading the chapter which comprises the topic of that session. This helps to maintain the general focus of the session, as well as providing some basic information to stimulate the discussion. (Experience, though, suggests that parents will participate actively in discussion even if they have not yet read the chapter, and that some parents will have read the entire book prior to the first or second session.)

Group facilitators should be thoroughly familiar with the content of the various chapters of *Guiding the Gifted Child* prior to beginning the group series, and should review each particular chapter prior to that session so that essential points can be emphasized and underscored during that group session. To aid facilitators in that process, the essential aspects of each chapter are outlined below. Some facilitators have photocopied and laminated the weekly key topics (putting each week on a separate index card) to take with them to the sessions as reminder notes. During the session, then, they might glance briefly at the card to remind themselves of the key topics which they hope to cover during that session.

The sequence of topics from week to week follows a reasonably natural progression and most often flows easily from one to the next. Likewise, the techniques and concepts of the later sessions generally build upon concepts that have been introduced in earlier sessions. These earlier concepts (e.g., "catching the child doing something right," "special time," "anticipatory praise") are continually re-emphasized throughout the remaining sessions. We encourage you to study the weekly key topic list to insure that you will be able to facilitate discussion of each item listed, including possible related issues, pros and cons, controversies, etc. You may also wish to make notes of additional key topics that you hope to add to those listed here (e.g., Dabrowski theory, asynchronous development, etc.).

WEEKLY KEY TOPICS

WEEK I—*Characteristics*
- Characteristics of gifted children can be quite diverse
- Terms "gifted," "talented," "high potential"
- Intelligence is not the same thing as achievement
- Styles of learning ("right brain/left brain")
- Different methods of measuring potential, intelligence and achievement
- School screening and identification plans (they may overlook some children)
- What I. Q. tests do (and do not) tell (multiple intelligences)
- Obtaining assessment (including a second opinion)

WEEK II—*Motivation*
- Start where the child is; transfer motivations
- Successive successes; anticipatory praise
- Recognize the child's needs; goal-setting
- Encouragement, not criticism (avoid sarcasm/ridicule)
- Importance of personal relationships
- Special time/special place
- Frequency of praise is more important than amount or duration

WEEK III—*Discipline*
- Discipline and limits are needed for all children
- We set limits because we care
- Discipline is different than punishment
- Avoid "no-win" struggles, nagging, "referential" speaking
- Encourage choices to develop self-esteem
- Ensure that choices are within limits

- Seek self-discipline
- Catch the child doing something right in self-discipline
- Frequency of consequences is more important than severity
- Use natural consequences where possible
- Limits that are set must be enforceable
- Avoid harsh, inconsistent punishment

WEEK IV—*Stress Management*

- Some stress (challenge) is desirable; learn to manage it
- What causes stress is self-talk
- Blame and irrational beliefs leave us helpless
- Importance of balancing self-talk; "bookkeeping error"
- Perfectionism (idealism to an excess)
- Importance of parents modeling positive self-talk
- Don't teach stress management skills during crisis times
- Immediate calming techniques (HALT); teaching meditation
- Using humor to induce perspective
- Socratic method of teaching (e.g., "How awful is it?")
- How we manage our own self-talk

WEEK V—*Depression*

- Re-label depression as anger; inward or frustrated anger
- Depression as self-blame ("hair shirt"); negative self-talk
- Cannot argue people out of depression
- Avoid "Pollyanna cheerleader" or belittling of their feelings
- Existential depression; meaning in life
- Importance of relationships and of physical touch
- Evaluating seriousness; considering suicide
- When and how to refer; getting professional help

WEEK VI—*Communication of Feelings*

- Communication cannot be forced; create the climate
- Active listening is communicating
- Accept the feelings (though not necessarily the behavior)
- Avoid "killer statements"
- Modeling a relationship; "I" statements ("When you...I...")
- Barriers to communication (fast pace of life, television, newspapers, computers, etc.)
- Self-disclosure begets self-disclosure
- Special times and special places enhance communication
- Emotional temperature readings

WEEK VII—*Peer Relations*

- Who are peers? Peers in what area?
- Several different peer groups are often needed
- Many friends or few? How many real friends do *we* have as adults?
- Special friendships are often intense
- Bright children have high expectations; may lack tolerance for others
- Leadership or bossiness? Teaching leadership skills
- Use role-playing to enhance understanding
- Time alone versus time with others; eminence requires time alone
- Is time alone by choice or due to lack of skills?
- Peer pressure at different ages (including peer pressure on adults)
- Self-directedness and self-confidence help one withstand peer pressure

WEEK VIII—*Sibling Rivalry*

- Kids rival for something, usually attention
- Importance of birth order (oldest, youngest, middle) roles
- Children adopt characteristic roles, seldom compete

- Important to help children expand their roles and to promote role overlap
- "Either/or" concepts of giftedness; "if he is, I'm not;" negative comparisons
- Competition/rivaling versus sibling synergy
- Parents remove themselves from squabbles
- Take the "sail out of the wind"

WEEK IX—*Tradition Breaking*

- Bright, creative children question traditions, rituals, rules
- Creativity always implies being non-traditional
- Breaking traditions always has a price tag
- Kohlberg's stages of moral development; more advanced is less traditional
- Traditions have a value (but can be overly binding)
- Traditions promote belongingness and predictable behaviors; tap root
- Family traditions; sense of sanctuary
- Importance of creating our own traditions starting now
- What we model for our children in tradition breaking

WEEK X—*Parent Relations*

- Stresses of parenting; setting parental priorities
- Reacting to the urgent rather than the important
- Special time for parents; recharging your own batteries
- Dual parent, single parent, step-parent issues; difficulties in blending families
- Importance of having house rules
- Need for communication and consistency (family huddle)
- Super-parent versus reality

These topics are, in general, covered consecutively week by week. At times, however, the immediacy of the needs of one or more parents in the group will require that a topic (or portion of that topic) be dealt with out of sequence. Therefore, the flow of the groups does not always run along a neatly organized, linear, or logical sequence. The parents' needs and concerns come first (much in the same way that we advocate that parents respond to the child's needs), and the group facilitators must remember to "start where the group is."

Some examples of intense immediate concerns which occur with especially high frequency are the topics of sibling rivalry and of depression. For example, a mother may slump in her chair, clearly distressed, and say, "My daughters are killing each other! If they last until Christmas without murder, it will be a miracle. Now, my husband and I are fighting because he says I cannot control the kids." It would hardly seem appropriate for the group leader to announce at this point that sibling relations will be covered in Week VIII, and that tonight will be focused only on the Week IV topic of Stress Management. Similarly, in the first few minutes of Week II, a clearly distressed father might reveal that he has just discovered a collection of his son's poems, all of which focus on topics of sadness, death and destruction. It would not be appropriate, then, for the group leader to say, "Just hold on there! We discuss depression in a few weeks."

Obviously, the group facilitators must provide support for the immediate distress and must be prepared to interject information about any of the various topics. This does not mean, however, that the entire session would necessarily be spent on that parent's concern (though certainly a substantial amount of time may be). Instead, the more immediate concern should be dealt with (perhaps even for some length of time), and then one or more of the topics to be covered in the week's session can be gracefully introduced in a manner that fits within the framework of the parent's concern. For example, the group's attention right now may be focused on an issue of sibling problems, but within that context, the concepts and techniques of special time, successive successes and anticipatory praise from the book chapter, *Motivation*, could be highlighted and re-woven to relate to sibling rivalry. Likewise, depression, death and suicide are certainly topics which demand prompt attention; however, they also have clear implications for issues in the relationship that exists (or does not exist) between the parents and the child, and this may be introduced at an appropriate point as a way of re-focusing the group on the current topic of *Communication of Feelings*.

This is not at all meant to imply a cavalier treatment of such a serious topic. Instead, it is a recognition that it is not always appropriate for the group to focus overly long (e.g., half of the session) on one family's concern or to attempt to work with a situation that might call for professional intervention. It might be better for that parent to talk privately with one of the co-facilitators after the group ends (or in cases of extreme distress, for one of the group facilitators to leave the group quietly with that parent). Remember, this is not a therapy group. However, the group *can* act as a wonderful clearing house of information and provide a strong amount of support for its troubled fellow member. More will be said later about these potential problem issues along with suggestions for handling them.

CHAPTER IV
What SENG Group Facilitators Do

"The art of being wise is the art of knowing what to overlook."
–William James

"'And what is as important as knowledge?' asked the mind. 'Caring, and seeing with the heart,' answered the soul."
–Flavia

"In all things we learn only from those we love."
–Goethe

"A leader is best when people barely know that he exists."
–Lao-Tzsu

GUIDELINES AND PRINCIPLES FOR LEADING SENG GROUPS

Essentially, the leaders of SENG guided parent support groups facilitate a process of discussion and learning. This process is non-confrontational and non-didactic and is predicated upon the belief that a desirable outcome will be achieved by facilitating the individual's own understanding of problems and possible answers. The behavior of the group leaders overall is non-directive in the sense that the facilitator starts where the group is—within the framework of the group topics (remember: choices within limits). Nonetheless, there are specific behaviors which the facilitators can and need to use that allow them to maintain control of the group. It is important for the leaders to use these behaviors to keep the train (i.e., intense parents) on the track; however, the parents themselves provide the energy and the impetus.

It would also be accurate to say that the group facilitators continually attempt to model the very behaviors that they hope the parents will adopt in interacting with their children. Thus, while the parents are provided information through the book, handouts and discussion, the group leaders' behaviors emphasize the positive aspects, highlight the relevance for a particular family, or re-frame a concept to enhance its relevance for the parents.

In general, the behaviors of the SENG parent group leaders are guided by the belief that desirable outcomes will be best achieved with relatively little lecturing by the co-leaders. The primary contributions of the facilitators will be ones of active listening, asking questions, creating a climate of acceptance and inquiry and facilitating thoughtful consideration of worthwhile ideas offered by parent members of the group. Within that climate established by the facilitators, the leaders emphasize, underscore, rephrase and provide options and alternatives, with emphasis being given to the "take-home" value of the discussions. Note that giving information is relatively low on the priority list of what facilitators do in the SENG parent groups.

To promote "take-home" value, parents are encouraged to *try* new behaviors, but within one of the few clear and specific limits set by the group leaders: namely, the facilitators strongly encourage the parents to attempt no more than two applications, techniques, or behaviors each week. This limit is important. Not only do these parents typically want all of the answers immediately, but it is also virtually impossible for any family to successfully implement more than two changes during the course of one week. Such careful limiting of goals is, in itself, deliberately part of the atmosphere created by the group leaders and generally helps to reduce the frantic sense of searching for solutions that many of these parents may show. (It is noteworthy that many of these parents may be impatiently perfectionistic in their approaches to parenting, as well as in other aspects of their life.) Likewise, this measured pace time-frame is essential for parents who have been parenting in a relative information vacuum and provides the parents with time to establish new expectations, as well as time for the changes to be integrated into the family life. The specific way in which the group leaders limit these goals and how they do so in a non-threatening fashion is described later.

Although the group facilitating style is accepting, non-confrontational and seemingly non-directive, the leaders do, in fact, exercise control over the group. The aim is for the leaders to control through unobtrusive "conducting," in much the same fashion that an orchestra leader conducts the assembled players. The facilitators flow with the group's discussion—emphasizing and encouraging some parts, ignoring other parts, getting everyone to participate and generally guiding without dominating. The leaders listen, model openness and warmth and encourage participation. They do not argue or get in power struggles with parents; they are not judgmental or evaluative, nor do they insist on successes by the parents. In essence, the group leaders model behaviors that they hope the parents will use with their children.

A key principal for group leaders is that, as much as possible, they must start where the parents are—informationally and emotionally—and then guide them to explore possible alternate perspectives and behaviors. For example, the facilitators may listen and accept the frustrations felt by the parents with regard to certain behaviors of their children. But then the facilitators can "normalize" for parents that many of the interactions within the families are the result of characteristics that are normal for talented children (see Table 1) and not simply because their children are "selfish" or "uncaring" or "bad." In addition to "starting where the parents are," the leaders repeatedly will attempt to "catch them doing something right" and will use "anticipatory praise" frequently during the group sessions. (These techniques are discussed in the *Motivation* chapter in *Guiding the Gifted Child*, as well as later in this manual.)

To be the expert is *not* the role of the SENG group leaders. No one has all of the answers to perfect parenting—particularly regarding those diverse children whom we call talented or gifted. Even where a lecturing approach might appear to be the easiest and most direct way of imparting knowledge, it is best avoided. For teachers who are accustomed to this modality, such an admonition may be difficult to follow. Lecturing and didactic teaching implies that *you* have more answers than the other people and also runs a risk of raising feelings of defensiveness, inadequacy and guilt. Remember the saying, "I'm always ready to learn. I'm just not always ready to be taught."

Parents who are training to become group facilitators sometimes tend to be overly quick with advice based on their own experiences which may be limited to only a few gifted children—their own. In the arena of parenting, it is important to remember that what worked for you and your family may not work in other families and may not fit with another family's history and traditions. Regarding parenting—particularly of exceptional children— there are few absolute truths or hard and fast rules. Instead, what the facilitators and other parents in the group have to offer are guidelines and a variety of "recipes" that appear to have worked in at least some other families. This, then, allows parents to select from among the child-rearing "recipes." Remember, even in the same family, what works for one child may not work for another.

Thus, even when parents ask for a specific answer (as often occurs in the initial sessions), it is generally best to socratically reflect the question back for the group to consider with statements such as: "What have others tried?", "What are the key issues involved?", "What do you suppose the outcome might be if...?", "What effect might that have on your relationship with the child?", or "How might that relate to the issues of self-esteem and self-management?" Such an approach prompts the group to think about the issues, alternatives and implications much more so than if the facilitator had simply answered the question.

Sometimes, in response to a direct question, the group leader might simply say, "I don't know. I know that some parents have tried..." or say (with a touch of absurd humor), "I had all the answers to parenting yesterday, but I laid them down somewhere and lost them." To not always have the answers, and to say as much, has proven to be a highly desirable approach in working with these parents. It also models for them a patient and open approach which they might wish to use with their children, who ask similarly complex and difficult questions. Accepting that one does not have all of the answers also removes much of the pressure from the group facilitators.

The primary task of the group is to promote discussion and exploration of the topics, to share information and to try new behaviors. Parents are encouraged to contribute and share knowledge and ideas. In this way, what they take home is theirs (because *they* selected it, and because it was generated from information which *they* contributed), and thus it is far more likely that ideas will be implemented than if the same ideas were imposed by an "expert."

Reluctance by parents to participate—something which, if it occurs, will be found in the first session—can be overcome by simply inviting all of the parents in the group to contribute only one or two words which they think best describe gifted children or their child in particular. Parents are able to do this without feeling uncomfortable, and the one or two words generated by the various parents in the group release many threads of behaviors and characteristics of gifted children which can be woven together. For example, eight or ten parents—each giving one word descriptors—inevitably illustrate the complexity of thinking and behaving exhibited by these children, the enormous differences among them as a group and the challenges that are experienced by parents and teachers of these children. A broad discussion such as this, especially at the beginning of the parent group series, also validates for parents the "normality" of their gifted child's difference. For parents who have not had opportunities for open discussion concering their children, this sharing is indeed a relief!

This is *not* to say that leaders do not provide some information. Leaders undoubtedly will share some of their own previously learned knowledge about matters such as sleep patterns, identification procedures, the differences and difficulties inherent in the right brain/left brain behavioral paradigm and learning styles, but they do so in the context of a natural flow of information. If a facilitator gives specific information (a two or three minute "mini-lecture"), it is important to end by drawing the group back into a discussion format with questions like, "What do others think?" With practice, leaders become adept at judging when it is appropriate to offer information, as compared with when it would be more constructive to let the parents talk. The facilitator can then simply underscore, emphasize and admire the good information and behaviors being offered by the parents in the group.

On occasion, however, parents sometimes reveal parenting behaviors which are quite unusual or which are just short of outright cruelty. On other occasions, a parent will sometimes make unwarranted attacks upon a school system or will engage in "teacher-bashing." Though it may be tempting to respond directly and confrontationally, group leaders are better advised to at least temporarily refrain from commenting or showing a judgmental nonverbal expression. Overt criticism, like confrontation and arguing (and certainly ridicule) are to be avoided—whatever one might think privately. Remember, you cannot argue, bludgeon, criticize, or ridicule insight into others. Also, it is important to remember that there will be opportunities later in the session for you to help parents consider different perspectives.

Often, the facilitator—at some later time in the session—can insert a different opinion or offer different information while talking to a different parent in the group. Our experience has been that, in the flow of the group process, two helpful things generally happen: either the group members themselves choose to comment and offer differing views, or during a later interaction between a leader and another parent, the opportunity arises for the facilitator to highlight different and more appropriate approaches and principles as they are being described by that parent.

One example of the indirect handling of such a situation might occur during a discussion on discipline in which a parent intensely and unhappily describes the number of wooden spoons broken on the backside of his recalcitrant seven-year-old in the past month. The group facilitators do not comment (nor do they smile, frown, or otherwise editorialize on the behavior); the revelation about such harsh punishment is ostensibly ignored by them. Typically, one or more parents in the group might question the force required to break one wooden spoon, let alone several, and wonder what alternatives might be tried. Even if parents are reluctant to make such direct comments, the very nature of the discussion at some time during the session will provide one of the co-facilitators an opportunity to comment aloud on the advantages of restraint in disciplining children and on the undesirable consequences of "harsh and inconsistent punishment," which has been shown to relate directly to later juvenile delinquency. These comments will not be made directly or confrontationally to the wooden-spoon-wielding parent, but there will be little doubt as to whom they are being referred.

Note that the parent was not directly attacked and, therefore, was not put in a position of having to "save face." Further, because the facilitator, while talking to another parent, was praising the advantages of restraint, this generally more appropriate approach was being highlighted and reinforced as one worthy of consideration by the spoon-wielding parent.

As emphasized in *Guiding the Gifted Child*, focus on the positive and on "successive successes" is recommended in most dealings with gifted children. It is also recommended for leaders in their dealings with parents. When a parent recounts even the most marginally appropriate behavior, a leader can readily reinforce this by saying, "Wow! I admire the way you did/said/tried that." This technique of "catching the parent doing something right" fosters the behaviors that parents *should* try with their children, as well as in their interactions with school personnel (who certainly need support and encouragement, too!).

The focus on the positive can be used even where parental behavior appears to be extreme. In virtually every situation, there is *something* that can be admired about the parent, which thus provides a place to start in encouraging the parent to progress toward even more positive directions. Remember, at least the parents care enough to attend the SENG parent group sessions and to share their views!

For example, the parent may say, "Jane is going to be a straight A student, the valedictorian of her school, go to Stanford, and graduate magna cum laude—and I will see to it that she does!" Jane is age four, and such a parent statement is clearly a bit extreme. Instead of "setting this parent straight," the leader's response could be, "I can tell you really care about Jane and you want the best for her." In addition, at some later point in the session, the leader will probably help focus the group at large on difficulties parents can encounter when they take a highly controlling approach with their children. For example, the leader might go on to say to the group at large, "How do we, as parents, keep our children heading toward high achievement without taking over their lives and getting into the damaging power struggles that can so often occur? How much do we push; when do we know to back off?"

Even though at times it may seem that very small progress is being made in a group, an emphasis on "successive successes" will support and shape steady movement toward goals, as well as encourage the parents' attempts. Remember, we change our behaviors most often in gradual, small steps; seldom do we make sudden radical changes.

Sometimes, the group leaders may use an approach of "anticipatory praise" to encourage and guide the parents' attempts, as well as to focus their awareness on principles which we hope they will bear in mind. In "anticipatory praise," you praise the behavior that you *want* to occur before it has occurred, and by praising it, make it more likely that it *will* occur. In the group, "anticipatory praise" usually occurs as a second part of a statement. That is, in the initial part of the statement, the facilitator recognizes, accepts, or admires the parent. In the second part, the facilitator gives anticipatory praise. For example, the group leader may say, "I can tell that you really want the best for your children, and I admire how you appreciate that a good relationship is inherent in achieving such long-term goals. I think it is wonderful that you will be listening so patiently and thoughtfully to your child's opinions as you go along so that you can foster that relationship."

Note that the last portion of the group leader's comment was praising what you would *like* the parent to do—namely, *listen to* rather than *impose upon* the child. Perhaps the parent had that in mind; perhaps not. The group facilitator simply gives the parent the benefit of the doubt and plunges ahead with a comment that highlights an important aspect for parents in relating to children.

For some group leaders, one of the most difficult tasks initially as a facilitator is keeping the group out of "deep and meaningful" analyses of behavioral cause and effect—that is, playing amateur psychotherapist. Psychologists and counselors who facilitate parent discussion groups can find it a strong temptation to delve into an individual parent's personal or family difficulties. In fact, it may tempt any leader when a parent reveals to the group some highly personal matter—which may or may not be related to his or her children. Certainly, marital, family, or other personal problems influence parent/child relations and are factors in a person's ability to be a caring and supportive parent. So the facilitators must use judgement about how much to let a parent share intensely personal experiences and should attempt where possible to generalize these experiences in order to focus the entire group on parent-child implications.

If a parent continues to reveal highly personal and emotionally-charged information (this does not happen often, but it does occur), the other group members sometimes begin to look uncomfortable, although most groups are surprisingly accepting. If the group seems to be uncomfortable, the leader, having listened empathetically, can insert into the conversation, "It sounds like there's a lot going on at work/in your marriage/with your physical health/in your own personal background these days. Perhaps we could meet for a few minutes after the group. I believe I may have some resources for you." The leader then uses both verbal and non-verbal techniques to focus on another person or a related or prior issue in the group.

On rare occasion, a parent may be so emotional that he or she may need a brief recess from the group. If so, one of the co-leaders (the importance of having more than one leader is emphasized here) will quietly step outside with the parent to talk for awhile. Then, both will rejoin the group, typically without further comment. This is discussed in more detail in *Chapter VIII*.

Popular psychology is not unknown to parents of gifted children. Sometimes a recent newspaper or magazine article can serve as a springboard to lead to relevant topics for the group. Inappropriate "pop-psych" or personal matters that would be more appropriate for a counseling group should generally be avoided or minimized. This can be done by actively encouraging the group to discuss various practical matters which impact the family life, as well as through raising questions about solutions to be tried. For example, a parent may announce that he administered a ten item personality test from a weekly magazine to his children, and the results suggested that his children were passive and dependent. The facilitator might re-focus the group by saying, "How independent do we want our children to be?" Another technique is to re-focus attention on a previously discussed topic (e.g., "That reminds me of one of the aspects of Tradition Breaking that we talked about earlier this evening. How do we encourage our children to feel connected, but yet not overly connected to us?"). Yet another is to anchor the discussion to the book the next time a brief pause occurs in the group conversation ("What did you think of the 'Praises Phrases' on page __ of the book?") and re-introduce the topic of the week.

To gracefully maintain control of SENG parent support groups will demand some conscious awareness by the group leader and is able to be done with ease only after a fair amount of practice. But facilitators can quickly learn ways to continually guide and re-focus the group by taking an individual's problem, complaint, or issue and generalizing to underlying or related issues that most parents must grapple with. For example, if Wendy is using the group for "therapy" on the subject of her relationship with her mother, the group leader might comment, "Wendy, that's an interesting example of how important our relationships are with our parents. (Note: Wendy has been acknowledged, and the importance of what she has been saying has been validated.) We talked last week about how, if we want good relationships, we must keep the lines of communication open with our children. How have you (Note: The facilitator is looking around the entire group.) found this working out for you during this past week with your children? (Note: The group's attention has been re-focused on parenting issues, and other members have been invited to share regarding the topic at hand.)"

Many of the behaviors for group leaders described until now have been verbal ones. In the last example, we pointed out what the facilitator was doing non-verbally (i.e., looking around the entire group). It is our experience that the non-verbal behaviors (postural, gestural and facial expressions) are at least as important as what is said, and perhaps even more important. Use of a variety of non-verbal techniques can allow the leader to focus attention on a group member, lessen the attention on another group member, emphasize a point being made, deflect a comment back to the group, provide encouragement and support for a particular parent and generally be in control of the group without being obtrusive. More will be said later about using eye contact, hand gestures, body posture and other non-verbal behaviors which are used to facilitate the SENG parent support groups.

SPECIFIC GROUP LEADER BEHAVIORS

Group facilitation is influenced by both verbal and non-verbal behaviors. It is important that the group facilitators be aware of and practice a variety of verbal and non-verbal behaviors that have proven quite helpful. Although initially practicing these specific behaviors may feel artificial, the behaviors quickly become part of the facilitator's repertoire. In past training sessions, SENG group facilitator trainees have indicated that it is extremely difficult initially for them to think about what they are doing while simultaneously thinking about the key points to be introduced, yet at the same time also thinking about what the parents are saying in the group. With practice, fortunately, trainees are able to quickly accomplish these three simultaneous tasks. (It also helps if you have more than one group facilitator, since you can be thinking and observing while your co-facilitator is speaking.)

The flow and momentum of the SENG parent groups will be assisted by group leaders who can "conduct" rather than "control," using both verbal and non-verbal techniques to facilitate the pattern of interactions between parents and to promote and reinforce the awareness of the key concepts. The technique of "conducting" depends on the skill of harmonizing the verbal and the non-verbal activity with the content being discussed. Sometimes this means harmonizing your non-verbal actions (gestures, facial expressions, posture) with your own verbalizations (e.g., shrugging your shoulders while you are saying, "That's a difficult question for parents to answer."). Other times, this means putting your non-verbal behaviors with the verbalizations of someone else who is speaking (e.g., silently applauding when a parent speaks of a new behavior that they tried which was successful).

The following specific suggestions are ones which trainees are encouraged to practice in a variety of interpersonal settings. Most of these SENG facilitator behaviors are focused on simply encouraging and reinforcing participation in the group, though they may also be used to add focus or to highlight or emphasize. As we have mentioned before, though, facilitator behaviors are sometimes needed to re-direct or even to dampen a parent's participation.

To assist in developing the array of conducting skills which SENG parent support group facilitators need, a scale of facilitator verbal behaviors is helpful. This scale describes a level of verbal activity which ranges from low verbal activity to moderate to marked activity. The following material was developed by Finesinger (1948) and applied to common group situations, but has been adapted slightly because it is so useful as a model of communicating skills for SENG facilitators.

LOW VERBAL ACTIVITY

Low verbal activity behaviors are quite safe ones for facilitators. Remember, it is difficult to *listen* oneself into trouble. Also, the more you talk, the less the parents talk.

These low verbal activity behavior techniques should be mastered first, since they are both powerful and non-intrusive, particularly when they are accompanied by the facilitator's non-verbal "conducting" behaviors. The guiding principle here is that "less is more." These brief verbalizations can allow the facilitator to elicit more information from the speaker, but in a way that is non-judgmental. Or they can allow the facilitator to underscore and emphasize a key point, but without making a speech about it.

Low verbal activity statements also allow the facilitator to conduct and direct the group without appearing to do so overtly as directing or lecturing the group. Because of this, these techniques allow the facilitator to better "start where the parent is" and to get a fairly clear picture of the parent's concerns and style of thinking in a form that is relatively free from outside influence. Table 5 lists some of the most useful specific low verbal activity behaviors.

TABLE 5. *Low Verbal Activity Behaviors*

- Articulate syllables (e.g., "Oh" or "Mmmm") or say a single word (e.g., "And...") with rising vocal inflection.

- Repeat the person's last word (or a key word) to provide an emphasis or focus on it (e.g., "Angry," "Alone"). This single word could be said as a statement or as a question.

- Use an incomplete statement that restates a key word and leaves it hanging (e.g., "Strong feelings lately...?", "But spanking...?", "And if he doesn't want to...?").

- Urge with a mild command (e.g., "Go on," "And then?", "So...").

- Use general questions directed at a topic (e.g., "You said something about stress?").

The low activity level techniques can be used repeatedly. Do not give up too soon. Use moderate or marked activity only for brief periods to highlight a principle, draw a connection, or to redirect the group when lesser activity levels haven't worked. Then, once again withdraw to the low activity level. Avoid lectures, lengthy explanations, or taking over the group (except briefly to highlight a point). Instead, as much as possible, let the parents do the talking while you underscore, emphasize and "catch the parents doing something right." You may want to use an "Amen" approach such as one sees in the "call and response" of African-American churches, in which speakers are literally encouraged while they are still speaking. For example, if a parent is describing some good attempts at reaching out to his son, you might simply mutter, "Wow, wow!" under your breath. Or similarly, you might even label a technique that the parent is exemplifying by softly saying, "Anticipatory praise!" as the parent talks about her interaction.

At the outset of a parent group meeting, the facilitator will need to be a little more active and usually will begin with a general question. Even here, though, a low activity level is recommended. The opening question should not be one that could be answered by a simple "Yes" or "No," and probably should not be a leading question which suggests the answer. For example, you probably would *not* want to start by asking, "Do gifted children have stress?" Instead, the facilitator might start with questions such as:

"Where should we start tonight?"

"How did your homework go?"

"What are particular stresses for gifted children?"

"Where would you like to start on Tradition Breaking?"

"What caught your attention in this week's book chapter?"

"What peer issues are gifted children likely to have?"

Or the facilitator may simply state the topic (e.g., "Motivation") and then look inquiringly around the group, extending an open hand in invitation to whomever wishes to participate. After their general introductory question or comment, the group facilitators can usually revert to a low activity level to facilitate and guide the group interactions.

When the parents speak, allow the group initially to "browse." Low verbal activity (e.g., "Mmm," "So...") or silence can be used as prompts to continue, as can several non-verbal techniques which will be discussed later. If a speaker hesitates or stops, the facilitator might wait a few seconds (or even longer) to give the speaker a chance to continue. Simultaneously, the facilitator might look or gesture to other parents to join in or comment. Or the facilitator might simply let the parent ponder what has just been said. (Note: Remember teacher "wait time," in which teachers intentionally wait before calling on a student.) Many parents will try to put the facilitator into the role of the "expert" and will look to the facilitator to have the answers and to respond directly to their questions. The facilitator wants the group to contemplate the issues and to empower the parents to attempt to figure out the answers on their own. If silence persists, the facilitator might introduce another non-leading question (as in the examples above) or direct a statement to the co-facilitator (e.g., "Comments like that make you appreciate the complexity of these issues with our children," or "It's important to take time to think, particularly about our priorities within our families.").

AVOID OR MINIMIZE IRRELEVANT TOPICS

A low level of facilitator verbal activity using the above techniques generally can help avoid or minimize irrelevant topics (e.g., the latest basketball scores) without using a higher level of verbal activity. If a parent introduces a topic that is irrelevant, it is certainly acceptable for the group facilitator to avoid reinforcing that comment. Show no interest in that discussion, take no lead and ask no questions. At most, a soft, noncommittal "Mmm" is generally sufficient, and non-verbal behaviors by the group facilitator (e.g., looking around the group) can usually redirect the focus to other group members. If necessary, the facilitator might pick up a prior comment from another parent or even introduce another general question.

FOCUS INTEREST ON TOPICS WHICH FURTHER THE GOAL

As soon as a parent mentions a word or an issue related to the topic of the evening, the facilitator can focus attention using a variety of low verbal activity techniques (or non-verbal gestures, such as a reaching out one's hand) to signal, "Go ahead, we're interested." Or the facilitator might simply lean forward, nod, raise eyebrows, or otherwise indicate interest. If a glance will do, say no more. Once again, use the less verbally active approach, remembering that "less is more." Articulate syllables (e.g., "Ah...", "Hmmm...", "Then...", "So...", "Well...", "But...", "And..."). If a single syllable or word will do, use it. Reinforce the inflection with an encouraging look; let your voice carry along. Avoid an error of finality, and instead convey a sense of incompleteness.

As noted previously, use repetition of a key word or an elaboration left as an incomplete sentence (e.g., "But when you punished...", "But on the other hand..."). If these fail (or if a particular topic aspect has not yet emerged), the facilitator might wish to go briefly to a moderate level of verbal activity by making a specific question about the topic at hand in a Socratic teaching approach, using moderate activity statements like, "What do we as adults really mean by peers?" or "If we have morale problems at our workplace, how do we handle them in that setting?"

MODERATE VERBAL ACTIVITY

In moderate verbal activity behaviors, the facilitator more openly intrudes into the group, offering information, summarizing, questioning, or reframing. These techniques are summarized in Table 6.

TABLE 6. *Moderate Verbal Activity Behaviors*
• General Socratic questions (e.g., What motivates us as adults?").
• Reframing statements (e.g., "That sounds like it could be creativity.").
• Introducing specific information (e.g., "There's an interesting theory about intensity called the Dabrowski 'over-excitabilities.' Dabrowski said...").
• Bridging statements (e.g., "That was similar to the concepts in Motivation in which we talked about frequency of consequences being more important than magnitude.").
• Summarizing statements (e.g., "We've covered a lot of ideas tonight— using 'I' statements, special places, special times, reflecting on feelings...").

Sometimes it is quite appropriate for the group facilitator to use a moderate level of verbal activity and even to "take the floor" for a period of up to a minute or two. Some situations where this would be appropriate are as follows.

"JUMPING LEVELS"

Focusing on the "here and now" (also known as "jumping levels") may be used to stimulate a sense of perspective. The facilitator focuses on the group process (e.g., "Why do you suppose it is difficult for people like us to talk about these topics?"), or the facilitator talks about adults in general as a way of jumping levels to demonstrate that issues for children often continue to be issues for adults (e.g., "How do we as adults handle peer pressures?" or "What have you noticed about your own sibling relations as adults, and how do sibling roles continue even into adulthood?"). Jumping levels re-frames a childhood issue in terms that allow the parents to get better perspective and understanding.

THE "MINI-LECTURE"

Use a "mini-lecture." Sometimes the group facilitator can take the floor for a brief period to impart information that otherwise might not be available. For example, the facilitator may need to describe in some detail the techniques of "special time" or "taking the sail out of the wind." Similarly, the group facilitators will need to be more active at the close of each session in describing the homework process of the groups and in summarizing or reviewing the key points that were discussed during the session.

"JUMP STARTING" THE GROUP

On rare occasions, groups will not begin interacting enthusiastically, or there will be a lull where a brief silence does not prompt further interaction. This may occur because of a variety of reasons. In such situations, the co-facilitators can begin talking to each other in a back and forth "on the other hand" fashion about a topic of the session. After three or four interchanges between facilitators, the parents will join in this rapid-fire interchange, and the facilitators can revert to a lower level of activity, allowing the parents to take the floor and thereby leaving the facilitators to underscore, emphasize, highlight, praise, etc.

SUMMARIZING STATEMENTS

Particularly at the end of the sessions (and sometimes at the opening of a session) it is helpful if the facilitator summarizes key concepts and issues. This also can allow the facilitator to elaborate on the information brought up in the session, as well as to particularize how these concepts and issues relate to the readings and to the parents' lives. Often, this can be done in a particularly effective fashion by simply stating a string of individual words and phrases (as contrasted with speaking in complete sentences), since the parents are mentally able to fill in the rest of the sentences extremely rapidly in their own minds.

MARKED VERBAL ACTIVITY

Marked or intrusive activity should be used rarely and with caution! Such methods, even when successful, tend to emphasize the facilitator's authority and omnipotence. When they are not successful, marked verbal activity behaviors can often leave feelings of inadequacy and guilt and may seriously strain the facilitator's relationship with the parents in the group. Examples of marked activity by the facilitator would include the following:

- A provocative and dramatic interpretation, such as, "I hear a lot of anger in how you relate to your child," and "I cannot help but wonder if these are not your issues rather than your child's issues!"

- Rapid challenging, such as, "I just don't understand that." "Now, think about that!" "That just doesn't fit, does it?"

- Particularly active reassurance, such as, "Having feelings and behaviors like that is not uncommon. A lot of people have told me things like that, and I don't think you need to worry about this much at all."

Lecturing, criticizing, arguing, or pontificating is virtually never appropriate. An example of this would be, "The experts in the field have developed the following six approaches which have been proven to help the classroom teacher in developing the potential of such children. You are wrong to question or challenge whether they are appropriate for your child."

Such statements are rarely appropriate. Extremely directive participation of the facilitator in the group should be avoided, except in the first session and perhaps the last two sessions. The first session does involve giving more information, and the last two sessions involve more activity by the facilitator to wrap up and pull together the gains that have been made by the group attendees. In addition, the group facilitators will generally want to try to help the group avoid opening up major new topics during the last session of the series, since there would not be time to adequately process those topics. Perhaps the only other time when marked verbal activity might be necessary is if it is used to re-direct the group focus in some major way. Even in that instance, it is important not to be too quick to do so and to remember to flow with, rather than fight against, the group.

Despite all of these cautions, it is still accurate to say that brief periods of marked verbal activity levels can nonetheless be helpful, as long as they are positive in tone. The leader can actively reassure the group by relating experiences or information to make points explicit and to give concrete suggestions. Or the leader can reinterpret or reframe a situation so that the parents can appreciate its positive aspects. Even so, it is important that facilitators continually monitor themselves to insure that they are not lecturing at the group and that they return to lower activity levels as soon as it is feasible.

PACING OF THE GROUP

The facilitators' control of the group process is overtly minimal; however, the subtle control of the group process is important and is clearly present. The role of the group facilitator is much like that of the conductor of an orchestra. The conductor gives some instructions and there is a printed score, but primarily, the conductor blends the group together and directs the players in a clear, though often unobtrusive, fashion. The conductor's approach optimizes the interactions within the group and helps to optimize variations on themes by encouraging different players (using non-verbal cues) to come forth at different times.

Many techniques already described are central to the process of conducting. In addition to those techniques which emphasize content, there are techniques which emphasize the behavioral and non-verbal style of the facilitator. Some particularly helpful techniques for pacing and facilitating the group are as follows:

- Eye contact should be spread around the group; it is important to avoid looking only at the person who is speaking. In fact, the facilitator should usually look at the speaker only briefly and then should look to the other parents to gauge their reactions and to invite their participation. Only periodically should the facilitator look back at the parent who is speaking, and then usually only for a brief time. Though this behavior may seem to be rude, it is an important aspect of conducting, even though it may feel awkward at first.

- Body posture by the facilitator can indicate openness, excitement and support, or it can indicate a relative lack of interest in a particular topic. Leaning forward in one's chair and leaning backward communicate different messages. Similarly, gazing reflectively at the ceiling can suggest that the topic is worthy of thought and consideration.

- Voice speed also controls the momentum of the group. Sometimes the SENG group facilitator may take over the floor and then slow the voice speed in order to make sure that the group members truly hear and appreciate the importance of a point being made. At other times, the facilitator may use a rapid speech rate to convey excitement.

- Hand gestures and facial expressions are extremely effective pantomime ways of under-scoring important points being made by another speaker, yet do not interrupt the parent who is speaking. Coordinate your gestures and facial expressions to reflect the speaker's content. This might involve raising eyebrows, looking surprised, giving a thumbs up sign, a shoulder shrug, etc.

Non-verbal behaviors are a powerful and concise means of communication. In the context of the SENG parent groups, non-verbal conducting is intrinsic to developing the group process. In order to optimize parent interactions, verbal interventions (as noted previously) are generally minimized except for brief intrusions. By contrast, non-verbal behaviors are generally maximized in order to actually invite parent participation, as well as to control or conduct those interactions.

Head nodding, facial expressions, hand movements and a wide array of expressive "Mmms" are combined with active monitoring of the group. Eye contact can invite contribution just as surely as a spoken invitation. A parent who is dominating the conversation can be dampened by not making eye contact or by a timely "shoulder block" from the leader. Taken to extremes, the leader can actually stop a speaker by physically raising a hand (like a policeman indicating "stop") to interrupt eye contact. An extension of an open hand will draw attention to the next contributor, as can an expectant head nod. Thumbs up or a theatrical silent clap can endorse, support and underscore the importance of an insight or success of a new behavior that has been attempted. Hands spread in a palm upwards gesture can convey that the issue being discussed is complex and can be viewed with many "on the other hand" viewpoints. All of these messages can be communicated, therefore, without interrupting the flow of conversation among the parents, but yet speed the discussion along while simultaneously underscoring and promoting a focus on various aspects of the group discussion.

Similarly, SENG group facilitators can use body language in situations to avoid being placed unduly in an "expert" role, in which they are being pressed to give concrete answers. An expressive shrug or a smiling facial set, combined with a hand gesture to invite the opinions of others, will assist the leader to remain separate from a verbal entanglement that would not be helpful.

The facilitators of the SENG groups monitor the parents continually. By glancing around, the facilitators maintain control of the process by observing the parents' body language, noting who is contributing, who is waiting to contribute and who needs encouragement to contribute. Usually, when one facilitator is speaking, the other facilitators are engaged in looking around at various group members, although this is also done somewhat while one of the parents is speaking. Experience has shown that the parents do not perceive such behavior as rude, but rather see it simply as redirecting their comments to the group at large.

Ideally, leaders function simultaneously at two levels—one level focuses on the content of what is being spoken, while the other facilitator observes the group process, including non-verbal behaviors. Conducting by the facilitator is thus a dual process of facilitation and observation. Conducting is best learned through role play and practice, and the learning curve for facilitator skills goes up rapidly.

CHAPTER V

Techniques that Group Leaders Model

"Leadership and learning are indispensable to each other."
–John F. Kennedy

"Example is the school of mankind, and they will learn at no other."
–Edmund Burke

"Kind words can be short and easy to speak, but their echoes are truly endless."

–Mother Teresa

"Whoever undertakes to set himself up as a judge of Truth and Knowledge is shipwrecked by the laughter of the Gods."
–Albert Einstein

Although several of these techniques have been briefly mentioned previously, the following specific techniques are essential to good facilitation of the SENG parent groups. Thus, more elaboration on them is given. Note that many of these techniques are exactly those that the parents read about in *Guiding The Gifted Child* and which they are encouraged to implement with their children. Sometimes the parents will notice (and may comment) that the facilitator is using a particular technique. This awareness is not a hindrance to using these approaches, and generally the facilitator might simply smile and agree with the parent's comment. In other words, these are not secret strategies to manipulate the parents. Rather, they are basic approaches that seem powerfully helpful and effective in a wide variety of human interactions.

ANTICIPATORY PRAISE

Praise the parent or child for what you would like them to do, rather than waiting for the action to occur in order to praise them. Through such anticipatory praise, you make it more likely that the person will engage in that behavior later.

Example: Carol begins talking about how her son is frequently moody and irritable, and she shows her own level of frustration rising with these mood swings. The group leader might comment, "I am impressed with how you use your own feelings to help you understand your child. It is excellent that you can really listen to Johnny and show him that you care how he feels and that his feelings are important to you."

Of course, talking with her son about his feelings was likely *not* exactly what Carol had in mind for Johnny. Now, however, she has been given a strategy for dealing with the problem, and has already received praise and encouragement for it. The likelihood of her actually listening to Johnny and talking with him in a non-confrontational way now has been markedly increased through the use of anticipatory praise.

Example: To a mother who becomes really irritable with her child who wants eight reasons why he should take a bath, you can say, "I know you'll find that things go much smoother this week as you practice the patience and limit setting skills we've been discussing."

CATCH SOMEONE DOING SOMETHING RIGHT

Focus on some positive aspect of a situation or behavior. Find *something* to encourage about the parent or child.

Example: The parent tells how angry he is with the school and how he abrasively talked to the principal in a way which you would not recommend. The facilitator might say, "You clearly care about getting the best education for your child and are willing to help make it happen. It will likely be important for you to have several meetings so that you can insure that you thoroughly understand the school's constraints. I know you will make sure that the principal knows that you really want to help and are not just an angry rabble-rouser."

Example: Fred is talking about an argument he had with his daughter during the week. His narrative emphasizes how he "did all of the wrong things." The group leader ignores these inappropriate actions and instead emphasizes the one thing he said which probably *was* helpful to his daughter. The leader momentarily interjects, "What you said to Julie was very important for her to hear. You told her very caringly how you felt about the situation, and you did so in a way in which she was able to hear you and understand your position. How can you build on that?"

Fred may well have made almost every mistake possible and, if he knows it, feels very badly. It will serve no real purpose to make him feel worse about himself and the situation. If he does not know that he has made many mistakes, it is quite unlikely that you can bludgeon insight into him. If, however, he can be shown that there was at least one positive feature to his handling of the situation, he will most likely commit that "positive" to his future repertoire.

SUCCESSIVE SUCCESSES

Focus not just on complete success, but on small, attainable steps. Encourage parents to set small, attainable goals, and give verbal reinforcement and encouragement to them for even the slightest movement in the right direction.

Probably the biggest mistake in our dealings with people is that we forget that frequency is more important than magnitude. Remember, five "smiley faces" given one at a time is far more effective than 20 "smiley faces" given all at once. Similarly, a "time-out" of five minutes on three different occasions is likely to be far more effective than one "time-out" of an hour. As the dog food companies have said for years, "Put it in small, bite size chunks!"

Thus, it is important for the facilitators to catch the parents doing something good in *small* steps, while simultaneously helping them set such attainable goals for their children as well as for themselves. Praise and encouragement is given for reaching the small steps taken successively toward the overall goal. Initially, the progress is often slow but rapidly increases with each session. It is easy for people to behave in ways which they already know. It is difficult to learn to engage in new behaviors.

REWARD RATHER THAN PUNISHMENT

Punishment only conveys what *not* to do rather than what *to* do and also dampens a relationship. As such, punishment is simply less effective than reward. In the group, the leaders model "reward, not punishment" through the reinforcement of positive behaviors by praising, admiring and making supportive comments, while simultaneously avoiding sarcasm, ridicule, condemnation, confrontation, or direct criticism.

"I admire the way you..." is very powerful language. Remember, one can virtually always find something to admire about any given parent. Find something to admire, perhaps the way he listened caringly to his child's problem.

Example: "I admire you for sharing that with the group. I know that it is sometimes difficult to try a different way of interacting with our children."

During the group, encourage the parents to find things to admire about their children and about their teachers. Talking about the technique, as well as modeling it, facilitates its adoption and widespread use by the parents. Particularly admire their *attempts* at new appropriate behaviors, rather than only the outcomes.

MEETING PARENTS "WHERE THEY ARE"

Expect progress, not perfection. Start by trying to understand the parents' behaviors and needs as related to where they are now. It is not particularly helpful to judgmentally expect them to be where *you* think they should be. Remember that they are doing what they are doing because it is what they know how to do and is reasonable to them at that time, given their background and knowledge. Listen with patience, and help them change gradually and in small increments.

Meeting people where they are is a basic underpinning of successive successes and builds on approximations of the desirable behaviors—but by starting wherever the parent might be in terms of ability and insight. Even when the parenting behavior being described appears to be significantly inappropriate, it may be possible to adopt a global interpretation by stating, "Trying to look at your children with fresh eyes can be hard. I admire your willingness to consider alternatives."

It is easier to offer such praise if leaders remember that parents do not wake up each day with the idea that they are deliberately going to wreck their children's lives. Parents come to the behaviors they show because of their own experiences and beliefs. As leaders, we must start with their belief systems and attempt to expand their knowledge with other possibilities, thereby allowing parents to choose from among new alternatives.

SOCRATIC QUESTIONING

Socrates believed that the most powerful learning tool was one's own answers to the questions asked and that the key was in the nature of the questions. Of course, it is not as simple as that. But essentially, it is through questions that answers can be sought. Thus, rather than directly answering a parent's question, facilitators typically redirect the question back to the parent or the group members to find an answer.

Group leaders will have many opportunities to frame questions to guide parents so that they will reflect upon their goals, their actions, their motives and the impact they might be having on their relationships with their children. Over time, leaders may repeatedly use questions such as:

"What have you tried?"

"How effective has it been in the long run?"

"What do you think Amelia was trying to convey to you? What do you think might happen if...?"

"Has anyone dealt with this situation? What would you recommend?"

"You've really made a point there. I'm wondering what would happen if you made a few changes?"

"I wonder why that did not get the response you wanted?"

"Do you think we are missing something here?"

"How do you suppose Ann felt when you said that?"

"Do you think we could generalize that comment you just made to other situations?"

The list of possibilities goes on. All of these questions require the parents to reflect upon their behaviors and upon cause and effect, but in a fashion that is non-confrontational.

In dealing with children of high intellect and ability, parents often find that the parent/child relationship can easily become embedded in control issues. Parents may get caught up in power struggles, and they may feel that they have few options other than attempting to exert even more control over their children. Direct attempts by the group leaders (or others) to persuade parents that there may be other alternatives is unlikely to be met with success. Socratic questioning, on the other hand, is more likely to be successful because of its non-confrontive nature that promotes reflective consideration.

The modeling of Socratic questioning by the facilitators often results in the parents adopting it in dealings with their children and can reduce power struggles. The group leaders usually will wish to openly encourage Socratic questioning, since it is a very powerful tool for parents of high ability children. Socratic questioning recognizes their input, avoids confrontation and blame and enables the children to logically think through their positions. As a result, Socratic questioning promotes children's self-management, helps them feel better about themselves and strengthens the parent-child relationship.

TURNING STATEMENTS INTO QUESTIONS

Sometimes a parent will offer a very opinionated or even dogmatic statement. Yet virtually every statement, particularly those concerning parenting children, has many *ifs, ands,* and *buts* that might modify it. It is important to encourage the parents to explore such alternatives. The group leader may wish to springboard from a statement to turn it into a question with comments such as:

"How might that be different for children of different ages?"

"Would that always be true in every situation?"

"If we were to apply that to ourselves as adults, would it be the same?"

Turning statements into questions is often especially useful once the group has become relatively cohesive and when group members are prepared to help each other rather than rely on the group leaders to initiate discussion.

RECOGNIZING THE FEELING RATHER THAN THE CONTENT

The intensity of parenting—particularly with talented children—often leads parents to express their feelings forcefully, and some parents seem to interject their feelings regardless of the content of their concern. The group facilitators may find it helpful to comment on the feeling or the level of intensity being demonstrated rather than the content of the issue. For example, the group facilitator might say:

"You really feel strongly about that!"

"I hear a lot of feeling there."

"I can tell that this is something that you do not take lightly."

By displaying sensitivity to the feelings being expressed, the group facilitators once again are modeling an important technique for the parents to use in their dealings with their youngsters where communication of feelings often becomes an issue. Such comments not only convey a sense of understanding, but also often avoid premature hardening of a position or even a confrontation (for example, when the speaker is making a challenging remark to the group facilitator).

HUMOR

If used with a little caution, humor can be very effective in a group to lighten the tone, develop perspective and keep the group "out of therapy." Humor is a major factor in helping persons maintain a sense of perspective and balance with regard to setting priorities in parenting (and in life generally). It is said that there is a fine line between tragedy and comedy, and that if you push a tragedy far enough, it becomes a comedy. Thus, a substantial amount of humor, particularly absurdities, can be inserted by the facilitators at various times in the sessions.

The goal is to help parents maintain a sense of perspective and to see that even serious situations can often be dealt with through humor, particularly helping those parents who tend to "awfulize" because of their intensity and idealism. Simultaneously, humor provides a very useful modeling exercise for the parents in interacting with their own children. Parents can see how humor may be used with children to manage problems and to help put their own problems in perspective.

Facilitators must be cautious, however, about the tone of their humor so that it does not come across as sarcasm or ridicule. Nor should humor be allowed to distract the group from the reasons which they are attending the group meetings. Certainly, we want each group member to feel that his or her problems are being taken seriously, but on the other hand, humor can communicate that others have similar problems, that the problems are not truly emergencies, etc. Often, one of the best ways to use humor is for the group leader to make statements about himself or herself (or about people in general) rather than about a particular group member.

METAPHORS, STORIES, FOLK-SAYINGS

Folk-sayings, metaphors and brief stories are extremely effective. Not only are they a non-confrontational way of conveying information, but they also tend to be far more memorable. Parents are more likely to remember the approaches and techniques illustrated by a folk-saying or story than if a technique is simply described. For example, the leader may say:

"When you're in the middle of a hurricane, it is not the best time to teach navigation skills."

"Bulls often charge when we wave flags at them."

Not only are these sayings more easily recalled by parents when they are subsequently dealing with their children, but these sayings also often become "catch phrases" for the group that are used time and again in subsequent group sessions. (For example, three sessions later, the group leader might simply say, "Are you waving the flag at a bull?") Such a few key words can be especially useful in giving parents reminders of an entire issue or a concept discussed previously.

Some examples of other useful metaphors and folk sayings are as follows:

"It sounds like you have a lot of pots on the stove."

"Apples never fall very far from the tree."

"Perhaps there are too many irons in the fire."

"When your battery is run down, you have nothing left to give."

"Sometimes you have to take the sail out of the wind. You are the sail; your child is the wind. Take yourself to the one sacred room in the house—the bathroom—and close and lock the door until the wind dies down."

"The child who burns his lips eats his soup more slowly."

"When we pick at a sore spot, it often makes it worse."

Sometimes it may be helpful for the group facilitator to tell a brief story or relate an event in order to make a point. It is strongly advised that these stories not be told as personal narratives about yourself or your own family (even if they happen to be), but instead should be related as, "One mother told me about...", "I remember a colleague telling me that...", etc. The important part is the message of the story, not that the story relates to you personally. In fact, it can be potentially detrimental to mention that the story comes from your own personal history. Some parents might rush to adopt your approach, because after all, you are the facilitator; other parents might reject it out of hand because they disagree with something else you said in another setting.

SHORT PHRASES AND SINGLE IDEA COMMENTS

One of the reasons metaphors and folk-sayings work so well is that they are brief. Remember the power of the low level of verbal activity. Rambling monologues seldom help (parents, like their children, quickly tune out), and such monologues should be avoided unless done for some quite particular reason. Group facilitators should make their comments pithy in order to keep the focus on the topic. The use of "Mmm," "Yes," "Oh?", repetition of a speaker's last word(s) in conjunction with voice inflection and body response—all of these can be very effective. They can be punctuation marks that encourage the speakers and support their ideas, usually without them even being aware that you are speaking. Because of the importance of these low verbal activity behaviors, we re-emphasize some examples.

- Stating key words or brief phrases which underline or sum up what a parent has just said (e.g., "Relationships are the key!", "Listening.")

- Unfinished statements (e.g., "You come home and...", "Because harsh punishment...", "On the other hand...")

- Reframing value statements into questions (e.g., "How much *should* children have to conform?")

- Reflect an especially appropriate word with inflection (e.g., "Rivalry?")

- Use background reinforcers in an "Amen" fashion (e.g., "Exactly!", "Yes!", "Terrific!")
- Reinforcing and emphasizing points (e.g., "Mmm," "Wow!", "Interesting!")

All of these techniques help facilitate the group discussion, and many of them additionally have the advantage of "catching the parent doing something right" as they attempt to gain understanding and/or change behaviors.

NORMALIZING

Because these parents have exceptional children, they often wonder if what they are experiencing or what their child is experiencing is "normal." This is particularly true for first-time parents. Group facilitators can often share basic parenting information or even developmental theory to help parents see that what they are experiencing is really quite normal, expected and not as awful as it might feel to them. Often, other group members serve this role spontaneously with, "I've been through that one, too."

Sometimes, however, an incident described by a parent has portions within it that do not necessarily seem quite normal. In such situations, the group facilitators can initially emphasize the portions of the incident which approximate the average. Such emphasis allows a contrast to emerge which helps the parents focus on the other aspects of the situation which do need special attention—but hopefully which also allow them to feel less overwhelmed.

What is being modeled by the facilitators is the necessity of reducing the tendency to "awfulize," along with an approach of dividing the problem into component parts. "Awfulizing" tends to generalize so that parents often forget that good behaviors or elements are also present. For example, "awfulizing" seems to occur often with these parents concerning school experiences of their children. Since school is so central in children's lives, it is particularly important to help parents continue to appreciate its positives in order to maintain perspective about whatever dissatisfactions they might have.

Normalizing through humor can also be very effective, especially when group cohesion has been established. For example, Janet's thinly disguised exasperation concerning her son's latest impetuous action of tap dancing on the hood of the family car might be less pervasively infuriating if the group facilitator could respond with "I bet the acoustics from the hood were wonderful! My goodness, that sounds like a creative, stage-struck youngster there!" Or when James says, "Talking to my children is like talking to a brick wall!" the leader might say with mock-serious intonation and a roll of the eyes, "My children *always* listen to every word I *say*!"

RE-FRAMING

Re-framing is a similar approach to normalizing. In one setting or framework a behavior may look quite unusual or even bizarre; in a different framework, however, that same behavior is far less unsettling. A child who appears bossy might also be viewed as displaying leadership ability. The impulsive interrupting of others could be seen as a lack of concern for others, or it could be viewed as emotional intensity or eagerness to participate.

Re-framing is not meant to minimize the seriousness of real problems. Instead, it is a way of helping parents not overreact to situations or blow matters out of proportion, but rather to maintain a perspective which allows them to emphasize their relationship with their children (the most important single aspect to be emphasized repeatedly). Situations which seem awful can be restated to allow them to be viewed as more positive in a different setting. Many ideas for re-framing will flow from the "Strengths" and "Problems" listed in Table 1.

SELECTIVE IGNORING

It is not possible to respond to everything that happens in a group. Indeed, not everything *should* be responded to. Sometimes the most appropriate response is *not* to respond. Instead, the group facilitator may wish to *redirect* the group focus, use silence, or ask a general question. Such ignoring may be particularly appropriate if a confrontation seems likely. Remember, "flow with rather than fight against."

ALLOWING STATEMENTS TO GO TEMPORARILY UNCHALLENGED

Parents of gifted children may often make provocative statements, perhaps because of their intensity. Facilitators should avoid getting drawn into power struggles and generally should not immediately challenge statements. Instead, some of the previous techniques may be used.

Provocative statements can be a particular problem if the facilitator is a teacher and parents begin "school bashing." Remember, not challenging a statement immediately does *not* mean you support it. There will be other, more effective ways to move the group away from anger and to help parents learn how to be less provocative.

SILENCE

Silence indicates that you are really listening and that you are inviting others to speak. It also gives the group time to process their own thoughts. Group members will fill the gap if leaders are not too quick to jump in; thus, silence can help promote group participation. Sometimes it is most appropriate for the facilitator simply to lean back and thoughtfully look at the ceiling to allow group members to reflect on the implications of what has just been said.

NON-VERBAL TECHNIQUES

Facial expressions, nodding, glances, gestures, postural changes, vocal inflection and intonation can be used to encourage a participant to share or to discourage a parent who is dominating the conversation. Often, it is helpful for facilitators to put *their* non-verbal behaviors (e.g., hand gestures, facial expressions) with what a parent is saying. You will note that those non-verbal techniques are emphasized throughout this manual.

SUMMARY COMMENTS ON LEADER TECHNIQUES

The techniques modeled by the group leaders are intrinsic and very important to the success of the group process and need to be practiced. They may not feel natural at the outset, but we have found them to be worth the practice. Remember, some of your most useful teaching and parenting behaviors were ones you had to learn and practice before they came naturally and comfortably.

These same techniques are also especially valuable as strategies for the parents. The verbal and non-verbal behaviors which facilitate the group process are essential components of the leader's repertoire and complement quite well the content that is discussed within the sessions themselves.

CHAPTER VI
End of Group Session Assignments

"Knowledge must come through action."
–Sophocles

"A journey of a thousand miles must begin with a single step."
–Lao-Tzsu

"Most people are more comfortable with old problems than new solutions."

–Anonymous

Approximately five to ten minutes before the scheduled end of each session, one of the group facilitators begins to pass around a stack of Weekly Session Evaluation sheets and also distributes a packet of small blank sheets of paper for homework. (Note: The homework sheets are distributed each week beginning at the end of the second parent group session and are not passed out at the end of the first session.) Each parent takes one Weekly Session Evaluation and one small blank homework sheet. These two sheets are passed around while the discussion is ongoing and without any initial comment or explanation. Often, this is done by one facilitator while discussion is occurring on the other side of the group circle. This action by the facilitators conveys two important cues: first, the session is about to end, and second, the parents are to reflect upon what has been discussed during the session and perhaps will need to take some actions.

HOMEWORK ASSIGNMENTS

The blank homework sheets are no larger than an index card (more typically they are about half the size of an index card) and are usually bright colors to set them apart. If the homework sheets are larger than this, parents sometimes feel that they must take on extensive work assignments.

When each parent has a piece of paper and there is a brief pause in the conversation, one of the facilitators explains the homework assignment. (Specific language for explaining homework is given in the next chapter in the section on "The Middle Sessions.") As explained by the facilitator (and reiterated every week), the parents are encouraged to identify for themselves *one or two* specific behaviors or approaches that they will try as a result of the session's discussion. Also at this time, the group facilitators may summarize, or ask the group to summarize, a variety of possible behaviors or strategies which have emerged during the session. This review serves as a useful summary which can remind the parents of the various possibilities which they can use for their homework.

The parents are asked to take the sheets home with them (they are not shown to the group facilitators) and to keep their homework assignment sheets accessible (purse, wallet, dressing table, etc.) so that they will be reminded during the week to actually try what they have written. To underscore the importance of the homework activities, the parents are also told that the facilitators will look forward next week to hearing about the results of the homework.

The homework task embodies several key principles of the SENG groups. Parents are encouraged to *try* new behaviors (i.e., focus on progress, not perfection). Parents are encouraged to implement the ideas and behaviors, rather than just *talk* about them. By limiting their focus to one or two behaviors, the parents are encouraged to be realistic in their expectations of what can be achieved in one week. The safety established by the emotional climate of the group provides a model of the acceptability of experiencing less than complete success. Homework activities are consistently referred to as something everyone in the group is to *try*.

The word "homework" is used purposefully, since it establishes a tie with their children's functioning in school. In the first couple of sessions, it is not uncommon for some parents to come to a session without having done their homework. Group facilitators then can say to the parents (in a gently teasing fashion), "And what do you say to your children when they don't do their homework?" The parents, then, get the message that perhaps they are expecting their children to "do what I say, not what l do," and a heightened sense of understanding their communication styles with their children often results. In addition, the homework emphasizes an expectation that parents should move toward behavioral change and makes explicit a basic aspect of family dynamics—namely, that if one member in a family changes, then other family members will be influenced to change also.

WEEKLY SESSION EVALUATIONS

The *Weekly Session Evaluation* form, shown in Table 7, likewise serves as a prompt for parents to review what has occurred during the session, and it asks three open-ended questions. The first question helps the parents focus on "take-home value." The second question serves a similar function, though its primary purpose is to help the group facilitators monitor the group regarding what is *not* being discussed or regarding any unexpressed concerns by the parents. Parents may feel much more at ease in jotting down a concern rather than expressing it verbally, particularly in the earlier sessions. The third question helps facilitators monitor the parents' perceptions of the group process generally. It is in the response to this last question that parents may raise concerns that perhaps "too much time was spent on one parent's problems" or "the group leaders need to talk more."

In contrast to the homework assignments which the parents do not show to the leaders, the weekly session evaluations are collected by the group facilitators. Parents are asked to complete these forms without signing their names and to place them in a pile on the table as they leave the session. Reading the evaluations after each session helps facilitators keep a finger on the pulse of the group.

The end of session weekly evaluations follow a rather predictable pattern in the first two weeks of the SENG parent support groups. The parents' responses to the second evaluation question (i.e., "What subjects or problems were not covered that you would like to discuss?") will read like a veritable laundry list. Many of these intense parents will seemingly want all possible information that could be imparted, and they want it now (if not yesterday). By the third or fourth session, however, the lists typically shorten to one or two matters, often those topics or concerns for which there simply was insufficient discussion time. Subsequent weekly end of session evaluations by the parents tend to be highly positive and to report successes with a markedly reduced listing of topics not covered.

Facilitators, of course, will want to use their judgment regarding which comments they may wish to respond to at the next parent group meeting. If a topic listed on the evaluation sheet will be covered in a subsequent session, then the facilitator might simply ignore it. Remember, you will have ten weeks with this group. If the group has already spent considerable time on the issue, the facilitator might want to comment only briefly and then move on. On the other hand, some statements by parents on the evaluation sheets may warrant more extensive comment by the facilitator (e.g., a question asked about specific topics like Dabrowski theory, asynchronous development, or the reliability/validity of individual intelligence tests). Other questions (e.g., Internet resources) may be handled by providing a handout or by suggesting that parents who are interested call or write another resource (e.g., National Resource Center on Gifted and Talented).

Besides helping the facilitators monitor the group dynamics, the evaluations may be used in other ways. Sometimes the facilitator may wish to open a session to review some unfinished business with, "On last week's evaluations, there was a question about _____. Can anyone comment on possible ways of handling such a situation?" This not only helps meet the concerns of the group, but also communicates to them that the evaluations are indeed read.

Finally, it should be noted once again that the facilitators are modeling behaviors which they want the parents to emulate. The weekly session evaluations convey an openness to feedback or even criticism, but do so in a way that is balanced between the positive and the negative.

TABLE 7. *Weekly Session Evaluation*

Topic: **Date:**

• What were the one or two ideas or techniques presented that seemed particularly helpful to you and your family?

• What subjects or problems were not covered that you would like to discuss?

• What other suggestions or comments might help us to improve our program?

FINAL SESSION EVALUATION (LAST WEEK)

During the last SENG parent group session, a different evaluation form is used. This final evaluation form is shown in Table 8. The *Parenting Sessions: Final Evaluation* form is distributed earlier in this session than were the weekly evaluation forms in order to allow sufficient time (approximately 15 minutes) for parents to contemplate their responses. As the *Parenting Sessions: Final Evaluation* forms are passed around the group, the facilitators encourage the parents to reflect on the entire ten session SENG parent group series with regard to how the SENG group has influenced them and their families. The final evaluation form additionally seeks input into the content, process and effects of the SENG parent group series and asks for recommendations which the facilitators might consider in the future.

What facilitators will find are glowing, testimonial-type statements as to the effectiveness of the program and to themselves as leaders. Though the SENG groups are not therapy groups, it is clear that they are extremely helpful. Some typical comments that have been given by parents to facilitators in previous SENG parent support groups are shown in Table 9, as well as at the front of this book. You, too, will receive comments like this. Take the praise; you will have earned it!

These final evaluations are often helpful in promoting a better understanding and appreciation by others of the importance of the need for SENG parent support groups. Particularly useful in this regard are the responses to the second question on the evaluation form (i.e., "How strongly would you recommend this support group for parents of gifted?"). Sharing copies of the final evaluations with your school's coordinator of gifted programs, principal or superintendent, or with a funding source can be an effective method of insuring continued support for your SENG parent support groups. As one administrator said after reviewing such evaluations, "I shan't question your participation in these groups again!"

TABLE 8. *Parenting Session: Final Evaluation*

Date:

• What situations with your child (children), either at home or at school, have been helped as a result of this group?

• How strongly would you recommend this support group for parents of gifted?

• Comments:

TABLE 9. *Typical Parents' Comments in Final Evaluations*

"The stress felt by my child because of being identified as gifted was a real problem. Because of the sessions, we've been able to identify ways to lessen the burden."

"Parenting is often a lonely job. It's very important to know that you're not alone."

"Because of the groups, I have tried to spend more time listening to my son with complete attention and reflecting back appreciation and respect for his feelings."

"I cannot emphasize enough what finding an arena for expressing and sharing experiences and concepts with other parents and the trained facilitator has done for me as a parent."

"We're lecturing less and talking more. My child is in the process of learning self-motivation rather than doing things under threat of punishment."

"I think I understand why my child acts the way he does many times, and I can better deal with him and his behavior. It has been so comforting to talk with other parents who are going through the same things we are going through."

"Communications have been opened with the school so that we are now working together to help solve problems."

CHAPTER VII

The Framework of the Group Sessions

"New ideas...are not born in a conforming environment."
–William Blake

"Minds are like parachutes—they only function when open."
–Thomas Dewar

"So little done; so much to do!"
–Cecil John Rhodes

GETTING STARTED
(THE INITIAL SESSION)

Prior to the initial session, you will already have done some publicity activities (see *Meeting Notice*, Table 10) to inform parents in your area about the upcoming SENG parent support groups, and parents will have completed a *Registration Form* such as that shown in Table 11. This pre-registration procedure will allow you to limit the size of the group to an effective number. We would encourage you to consider advertising the SENG parent groups quite broadly and that you not limit participation only to parents whose children have been "school-certified" as gifted. Many underachieving gifted children are overlooked by schools, and we have found that when parents think that their children are gifted, they are usually correct. Even if the parents are not correct in their beliefs, a few sessions in the SENG group listening to other parents will help them to make a more realistic appraisal.

Our experience suggests that the minimum group size should be four families; the maximum should be fifteen families. This usually results in from six to twenty actual persons in addition to the group facilitators. A group larger than this does not allow sufficient participation by all of the parents. If more parents are interested, you can take their names and addresses and tell them that you will put them on a waiting list for the next series of meetings. Additional specific information and considerations regarding publicity and planning (e.g., when and where to hold the groups) are presented in *Chapter IX: The Action Plan* and in *Appendix A: Planning Checklist for Parent Groups*.

It is strongly preferred that you arrange for the parents to receive a copy of *Guiding the Gifted Child* prior to the first parent group meeting. This can be done by sending the book by mail, or the books can be delivered to the parents' homes. Direct delivery to the door is an extremely powerful way of communicating to these parents that you do, indeed, want their presence—a message that seems to be particularly important for minority or disadvantaged families. Whether mailed or delivered, these books are accompanied by a confirmation letter which includes reading assignments, meeting dates and directions to the meeting locale. A *Sample Confirmation Letter* is shown in Table 12.

TABLE 10. *Meeting Notice*
ATTENTION: PARENTS

What:	Guided Discussion Group for Parents of Bright/ Talented/Gifted Students (Series of ten sessions)
When:	Tuesdays, February 9, 199__–April 13, 199__ 9:30 a.m.–11:00 a.m.
Where:	Public Library, Main Meeting Room, 123 N. Main Street
Co-Facilitators:	Maria Sanchez, Gifted/Talented Coordinator; Lee Ming, Parent of Gifted Child

TABLE 10. *Meeting Notice* (cont'd)

Cost: $30.00 (Covers cost of the book, *Guiding The Gifted Child*, and ten sessions for one or two parents/significant adults)
$18.00 for those who already have *Guiding The Gifted Child*

Registration Deadline:
Tuesday, February 2, 199__ (Register early; class size is limited)

Session Topics:

1. Identification
2. Motivation
3. Discipline
4. Stress Management
5. Depression
6. Communication of Feelings
7. Peer Relationships
8. Sibling Relationships
9. Tradition Breaking
10. Parent Relationships

Objectives:

• Establish an environment where parents of talented children can receive support, guidance and professional advice through discussion with other parents and trained leaders.

• Develop parenting skills to nurture the self-concept and emotional development of talented children and their families.

What Past Participants Have Said:

• "The class and book have been a life saver! I can't say enough good about them and feel that every parent should have the opportunity to be in a SENG group!"

• "I do not feel as alone now."

• "I came into this class a little nervous and wondering what I would learn, just like everyone else. I'm leaving it knowing that I have made some good friendships and have gained a lot of knowledge about myself, my child, and how he perceives the world."

• "My child's a happier child, my family a healthier family, and I'm a better person as a result of the group. Thank you!"

How to Register: Complete the attached Registration Form and return it to Maria Sanchez, P.O. Box 5003, Des Moines, IA 88866 (Phone: 555-1234)

TABLE 11. *Registration Form*

SENG PARENT SUPPORT GROUP

Name: _____ Phone: _____ (Home)

Address: _____ Phone: _____ (Work)

Child Information (Please indicate by * any children who have been identified as gifted)

Name of Child	Age	Sex	Grade	School

How did you learn about this group?

_____

We will send you a confirmation letter shortly, along with a copy of *Guiding The Gifted Child*. This will allow you to read some of the book, if you wish, even before the first group meeting. We encourage the two adults who are most central in the child's life both to attend the group meetings. It helps to have someone with whom you can discuss the ideas. In this way, you are more likely to get the most benefit from the group meetings. If you have any questions, please call Maria Sanchez at 555-1234. We look forward to seeing you at the group meetings.

Please make your check payable to Des Moines Public Schools. Enclosed is: (check one)

_____ $30.00—covers the cost for two people and *Guiding the Gifted Child*, or

_____ $18.00—covers the cost for two people (I already have *Guiding the Gifted Child*)

TABLE 12. *Sample Confirmation Letter*

January, 199_

Welcome to the guided discussion groups for parents of able, bright, creative students. Morning groups will begin Tuesday, February 2, 199_, 9:30 a.m. - 11:30 a.m., West Des Moines Schools' Conference Center, 713 Eighth Street, WDM, just south of Grand on Eighth Street. Enter off of the parking lot which is on the east side of Eighth Street. The receptionist will direct you to the meeting room.

Evening groups will also begin on Tuesday, February 2, 199_, 7:00 p.m.–8:30 p.m., in the activity room at Beaverdale Estates Retirement Center, 4610 Douglas Avenue. (Just west of Beaver on Douglas Avenue.) Enter the front door facing Douglas Avenue. The meeting room is to the back and right off the main lobby.

You might enjoy browsing through *Guiding the Gifted Child*, then reading *Chapters I* and *II* as a general introduction. Prior to each session, please read the assigned chapter in depth dealing with the discussion topic for that week.

Date	Chapter	Topic	Page
February 2	III	Characteristics	45
February 9	IV	Motivation	63
February 16	V	Discipline	83
February 23	VI	Stress Management	107
March 2	XI	Depression	191
March 9	VII	Communication of Feelings	127
March 16	VIII	Peer Relationships	145
March 30	IX	Sibling Relationships	161
April 6	X	Tradition Breaking	177
April 13	XII	Parent Relationships	205

If you have any questions, please call me at 292-7910.

Sincerely,

Anna Hernandez

The parent groups should be located in a "user-friendly" setting that is convenient and which allows the parents and facilitators to sit in a circle *without* a table in the middle. Note that the facilitators do *not* stand, and that they sit approximately across from each other. More will be said about this and other details in the *Action Plan* section which is presented later. As they arrive, each parent is given a name tag (written ahead of time). The facilitator may want to put the name tags in a plastic case so they can be retained for each session. (This also is an efficient way in subsequent sessions of noting which parents may have missed a particular session.)

As the parents arrive for the first session, introducing them individually to the "lending library" gives them an opportunity to browse. The lending library consists of a variety of books (such as those listed in *Appendix B— Books for Families with Gifted Children*) which the facilitators have collected and which are displayed on a table somewhere in the meeting room. The parent group attendees are told that they can borrow these books free of charge. A sign up sheet is placed next to the books on an adjacent table. The parents simply sign out the books, indicating their names and the date, and then cross that off when they return the book. The lending library allows parents who have children with special issues to explore topics on their own, as well as helps them to expand their base of information about gifted children which they often bring back to the group sessions. This gives parents something productive to do during a time that otherwise might be uncomfortable silence while waiting for the group to begin.

When the group is seated and the starting time has arrived, one of the group facilitators begins by welcoming the attendees, briefly introducing himself/herself and explaining what the groups are and what they are not. It is important to reassure the parents that these are not therapy groups, nor "gripe groups," nor advocacy groups, but are a place to "swap parenting recipes." The facilitator also might add that the SENG group is a place where it is alright to brag about your child. At the same time, the facilitator might wish to remind the parents that parenting is not without problems, particularly with regard to high potential children.

At this point, the group facilitator also might wish to "apologize" for using the term "gifted," because it carries such an emotional charge for many people, and because the term does not do justice to conveying the complexity, types and varieties of these children. As a facilitator, you will find that the term "gifted" often has some negative connotations for many parents, and it will help if you publicly recognize your own discomfort at the outset of the groups. The facilitator may then suggest that there are many terms which people use to describe gifted children. The terms "talented," "high potential," or "able learner" seem more widely acceptable, though "gifted" is the term that is currently used in literature and research these days.

The SENG facilitator should then structure the group process by telling the parents what will be done during that evening's session. The facilitator may say something such as the following:

"We will be meeting for ten sessions, each of which is focused around a particular topic. Each topic corresponds to a chapter in *Guiding the Gifted Child*. Each of you should have a copy. As we go from week to week, please read the chapter before the meeting on that topic so that you will get the most out of the session. I hope you will be able to attend all of the sessions.

"It would be good if the two most significant adults in the child's life could come to each session, although I know that this may not always be possible. This might be parents, grandparents, uncles, or even landlords or neighbors. Our experience has shown that it helps to have someone with whom you can discuss ideas after the group sessions.

"Tonight, the topic is on characteristics of gifted children, and we will try to share information with you about typical characteristics and about identifying those children who we call bright, talented, gifted, or high potential. In this first session, the facilitators will probably do a good bit of the talking. In later sessions, though, we will probably be somewhat quieter. We want this to be your group, and we will add what we can.

"First, though, it's important to know a bit about each other. Even though this will take some time, let's introduce ourselves. As we go around, introduce yourself and tell us a little about your children and what has brought you to the group. I will begin. My name is Michael Hall, and I have two daughters, ages five and eight..."

This allows the facilitator to speak first in order to model introductions as to content and length and gives the parents some idea of what they themselves might say as they begin their new group experience. Introducing oneself is part of the agenda for the first SENG session. Several points deserve special comment. First, the facilitator generally reveals how many children he/she has, their ages, and perhaps a short comment about some of the characteristics of each that typifies gifted children (e.g., "Amy has always been passionate about art, but in the rest of her schoolwork she does well or poorly depending on whether she likes the teacher."). Such self-disclosure is more than leaders generally do in other types of groups, but it works well here. (Note, however, that self-disclosure beyond this amount is *not* recommended for facilitators. Extensive self-disclosure is not needed and can make the parents feel uncomfortable.) If you are a facilitator who does not have children, then we recommend that you simply say, "I'm John Adams. I don't have any children, but I have learned a lot from other parents who have gifted children, and I'm looking forward to sharing that with you, as well as learning even more from you. And I do have a gifted nephew."

Second, it helps to point out to the group at the outset that the introduction process may take quite a bit of time, but that the introductions are an important part of the group. Third, after the facilitator introduces himself/herself, the parent sitting adjacent is invited (usually non-verbally by means of a simple extension of the facilitator's hand) to go next. Note that the facilitator will have a choice of whether to start with the parent seated to the right or the parent seated to the left. The choice usually depends on the facilitator's initial impressions as to which parent might be most comfortable in offering helpful information to the group.

Fourth, as the introductions go around the circle, every parent attending should be encouraged (verbally or non-verbally) to speak. Sometimes husbands are quite willing to let their wives speak for them concerning the family ("I'm Margaret's husband, and she's already said it all."). Getting them to speak at this stage, even minimally, will enhance their participation in subsequent sessions. Fifth, as the parents introduce themselves in turn, a facilitator might offer support, understanding, or a tidbit of information about gifted children by adding some brief comment after a parent's introduction, such as:

"Yes, that often seems to be characteristic of bright children."

"It sounds like you have your hands full."

"I admire your way of describing."

"It's interesting that you said she seems so excessive. Gifted children are intense, aren't they?"

Not only do such facilitator comments communicate a supportive environment, but also that the team "gifted" covers a wide range of abilities and diverse behaviors.

As the parents offer their introductory remarks, it is common to observe other parents smiling, nudging each other, or in some other fashion indicating that they recognize and identify with what the other parents are saying. The group facilitators should non-verbally acknowledge this as the introductions proceed through such behaviors as smiling at these other parents, nodding a head toward them, silently extending an open hand, etc. (Remember, you will be looking *not* just at the parent who is speaking, but will be glancing around at other parents during each parent's introduction.)

After the parents have introduced themselves, the facilitator may wish to further promote the parents' participation by asking them to brainstorm an adjective that describes their understanding of a "gifted child." This approach is non-threatening and can serve as a springboard for introducing concepts from the literature which describes talented and gifted children, along with some of the more common approaches to identifying these children.

The discussion in this initial session will often subsequently go into areas such as how different school systems vary in their approaches to identification, the difficulties of identifying potential at an early age, the difference between potential and achievement, or the relative merits of teacher nomination, parent nomination, group achievement tests, behavior checklists, etc. Sometimes, parents at this stage will want to complain about or attack the school systems. Though some of their specific criticisms can be ignored, it may be important for the facilitator to occasionally remind the group that schools reflect what society demands and generally are doing the best that they can at this time. Along with this, facilitators can point out that, although appropriate schooling is certainly desirable, research suggests that family and parenting are more important in the long-term outcome of gifted children than is school. This can help emphasize the need to focus on parenting and family issues.

During the first group discussion, one or more parents virtually always has children who are not living up to their potential academically. This sets the stage very nicely for the next week's topic of Motivation.

Approximately ten minutes before the ending time, the Weekly Session Evaluations are distributed, and the purpose of the evaluation sheets is explained to the parents. The homework sheets are not used at the first session, but are used in all other subsequent sessions.

At this time, it is also helpful to remind the parents of the availability and purpose of the lending library explained earlier. The facilitator, at various times during the SENG parent group series, also can encourage parents to share with the group some things which they may have read that had meaning for them.

If the facilitators have not already talked about confidentiality within the group, the end of the first session is a good time to do so. Obviously, the facilitators cannot guarantee confidentiality, but they can encourage the SENG group members to respect the privacy of others in the group and to use appropriate judgment. Facilitators may also wish to talk here about whether the parents are willing to share their names and addresses with other parents in this group. Typically, we will say, "If there are no objections, we would like to bring next time a list of the names and addresses of parents in this group in case you want to be in touch during the week to swap ideas, to arrange for rides, or whatever. If you would rather not have your name and address on this list, please let one of the facilitators know either after the session or some time during the week."

After these explanations, it is time to end the group session. The group facilitators should push back their chairs, stand and begin to gather up their materials. Without these non-verbal cues, the group otherwise is likely to continue its discussion. Even after the facilitators leave the room, it is not uncommon to find parents continuing to meet in small groups and to talk informally—sometimes out in the parking lot in very inclement weather!

THE MIDDLE SESSIONS

The name tags continue to be used for each session. (The leaders also wear name tags.) Some facilitators have found it helpful to collect the name tags after the first session and to have them on a tray from which the attendees can pick up their own tag at each session. This makes it easy to ascertain who is absent. Each week, the facilitators bring their copies of *Guiding The Gifted Child,* not only as a way of emphasizing the importance of having read the book, but also so that they can refer to it should questions arise.

In opening the middle sessions, the group facilitators may say such things as:

"Where would you like to begin today?"

"What particular parts of the chapter seemed to speak to you?"

"What questions have arisen for you since last time?"

Or simply, *"Sibling Relations."*

In the third session (and each week thereafter) it is often advisable for facilitators early in the session to ask, "How have things gone with your homework?" It is only possible to do this, however, at the third session since you will not have explained the homework until the end of the second session (Motivation). Homework is explained to the parents as follows:

"We want the SENG groups to have take-home value. Though it is nice to talk about ideas, it is most important for you to take home some ideas that you can apply. Think back on what we talked about this evening—perhaps catching the child doing something right, successive successes, anticipatory praise, etc.—and see what one or two ideas you would like to try this week. Limit it to only one, or perhaps two, that you will take home and try. Write them on your slip of paper. Do not show the paper to us, but put it in your purse, on your dresser, or someplace where you will find it during the week to remind you of what you are going to try. Then, next week, we would like to hear what you have tried, what worked, what did not work, what almost seemed to work and what fine-tuning might be needed. We will look forward to hearing what you tried and what happened."

This explanation of homework focuses the parents' attention on the various key points that were covered, asks them to make the techniques specific to their own lives and encourages them to attempt these techniques. Also, notice that the instructions specifically indicate that some techniques may not work the first time that they are applied and may need adjustments. This is an important aspect, since many parents will have tried a great number of techniques, though usually only for a short while, and these parents may be prone to being quickly disappointed if techniques do not work immediately.

Once each session's group discussion is started, the group facilitators will use verbal and non-verbal techniques to conduct the interactions and to weave the key concepts of the topic into the discussion. Generally, the parents will stay on the topic of the session, since the sequence of topics is a natural progression. Even so, some digressions will occur. It is acceptable to let the group wander in its discussion for a short while until the facilitators can ascertain whether the digression is a matter of some urgency to one or more members of the group, thereby needing more immediate attention. Usually though, after a short while, the group facilitators are able to tie into the discussion the concepts from the chapter of the book being discussed. Some of the more frequent ways of doing this are:

"It's interesting you would say that, because that ties in with _____."

"That's a wonderful example of _____ which was talked about in the chapter."

"I wonder if the technique of _____, which was described in the book chapter, would fit in this situation?"

If the group has wandered far off the topic, however, or if there is a particularly dominant group member, it may be necessary to use what has been called the "boom-boom" technique to re-orient the group. That is, the facilitator may acknowledge one of the parent's statements, but then that facilitator makes a series of succeeding statements—each off at a slight tangent—which eventuate in allowing the facilitator to reintroduce the topic or concept desired. The reason that it is called a "boom-boom" technique (besides being memorable) is that it comes from the following story:

Uncle Harold loved to talk about war stories, but his family was quite fed up with hearing the same stories, even though they liked Uncle Harold. One Thanksgiving, the family decided that they would do everything they could to *not* provide Uncle Harold with an opportunity to bore them with his war stories and agreed to not discuss anything remotely related to war or fighting. Before too long, Uncle Harold found himself fidgeting and looking for an opportunity. Getting up, he turned on the television to Macy's Thanksgiving Day Parade. Uncle Harold said, "Oh, look at the band. I love bands, particularly the bass drums. I like the bass drums because they go 'boom-boom.' 'Boom-boom.' Speaking of war, did I ever tell you about... .'"

Hopefully the facilitators will be more graceful than Uncle Harold. Nonetheless, the point is made. Sometimes it is necessary to "boom-boom" the group to re-orient the topic.

Each of the middle sessions is brought to a close by distributing the evaluation sheets and the homework sheets about ten minutes prior to the closing time. The instructions for homework and evaluation are briefly reviewed each week as a way of summarizing the key points and focusing on take-home value for the parents.

Usually by the third week, parents are bringing in success stories in which they have attempted some techniques and found them to be quite helpful. These opportunities should be openly supported and nurtured avidly by the facilitators. Such support and emphasis serve to encourage the other parents to attempt their own behavioral changes, and parents eagerly begin supporting and congratulating each other.

Some facilitators have varied the usual group procedure in the third week because the topic is Discipline, which is a topic that varies dramatically depending on the age of the child being discussed. Since the groups usually have parents of children of various ages, the group may spend only ten or fifteen minutes together as a whole and then divide into two sub-groups (parents of older and parents of younger children). The discipline issues are often so different that the parents welcome this specific opportunity. The two sub-groups reconvene about five to ten minutes before time to end the session. Parents who are reluctant to speak in the larger group may find it more comfortable to begin sharing in the smaller group setting.

Generally, as the sessions progress, the group's noise level increases steadily. The parents' enthusiasm and eagerness synergize as they acquire more techniques, attempt changes and experience the support and perspective provided by the facilitators and the other parents. Seldom is it necessary to point out to them that gaining just one or two new ideas in the course of a day makes that a very good day.

THE FINAL SESSION

As mentioned previously in this manual, the group facilitators are much more active during the final session than during the middle sessions. This is *not* a time to open up new areas, but rather to bring them to a conclusion. During the final session, it is helpful to ask the parents to reflect on how they and their families were when they started the series and to compare that to how their families are functioning at this time. The group facilitators should also comment on the amount of growth that they have seen (usually the comments are made to the group as a whole and in generalities, rather than focusing the comments on particular individuals).

This is a chance for parents to consolidate whatever gains have been made, and the facilitators can conclude the series leaving the parents with a strong sense of accomplishment and hope for the future. The facilitator will likely be much more active than in prior sessions and will occupy much more of the floor time in order to pull together the threads that have been woven over the ten weeks, encouraging the parents to continue on the paths which they have begun. This also is a time to point out to the parents that some of them may wish to return to attend SENG parent groups in the future, when their children are older and in different developmental stages, or just to get a "booster." It is not at all uncommon for parents to return, some even two or three times.

Often, parents are reluctant to terminate the ten session series, and they may ask for an extension. Our experience has been that ten sessions is as long as parents can reasonably commit to attending reliably. Sometimes the parents also will ask about a reunion. Again, our experience suggests that it is certainly fine if the parents wish to arrange for such a reunion, but the facilitators probably should not be directly involved in organizing such a reunion. At the last session, facilitators may wish to remind the parents to get phone numbers from parents with whom they wish to stay in touch.

One idea that often works well is to suggest at the next to last session that parents bring pictures of their children for the last session. The parents like putting a face with the stories they have heard about the child, and sharing these snapshots is universally enjoyed.

CHAPTER VIII
Potential Problems

"Within each problem lies the seeds to its solution."
    –American Proverb

"You can complain because roses have thorns, or you can rejoice because thorns have roses."
    –Ziggy, by Tom Wilson

Generally, the SENG groups go smoothly with typical ebbs and flows. Sometimes, though, a parent's behavior can create problems for the group. The most frequently seen problems and specific suggestions for handling them are described in this chapter. In general, facilitators can rely on the group to prevent or ameliorate problems. It is also important to keep in mind that problems which occur one week may not occur in subsequent weeks, and that over a ten week period, parents are likely to grow and change because of the groups. And remember, as a facilitator, you don't have to solve everyone's problems.

THE DOMINATING GROUP MEMBER

Sometimes a parent will tend to monopolize the conversation, either through telling stories about his/her own family or through trying to dominate the other parents as a "know-it-all." Facilitators wonder how long they should stay with one parent's topic. Generally, they will want to listen respectfully, particularly to ascertain whether what is being talked about is of interest to the group or is really a matter of seriousness that does need the group's attention for a substantial amount of time. One guideline is to glance around the group to see if the group members seem to be interested and concerned. If so, then let the group continue on its course. If the group members are beginning to show signs of boredom or restlessness, then the facilitator will want to engage in some behaviors to help control the dominating group member, but without "rising to the bait" of any provocative statements that may be offered by the dominating group member.

It is important that the facilitator not reinforce the dominating group member either verbally or non-verbally. The facilitator's gaze should be directed away from the dominating group member and toward other group members. Non-verbal behavior, such as a "shoulder block," might also be used to avoid reinforcing more dominating behavior. When the facilitators are able to get the floor, they can make a related statement that helps to refocus the group on the topic at hand (perhaps using the "boom-boom" technique), and then culminate in a general question that is directed toward members of the group sitting opposite to the dominating group member.

In the next session, it is often helpful if one of the facilitators sits directly adjacent to the dominating group member. This simple action is a strong controlling force because it reduces the eye contact that invites speaking, and it enhances the effectiveness of the "shoulder block." In addition, the group leader might make an indirect opening comment of anticipatory praise, such as, "Tonight we are looking forward to hearing from everyone about the topic."

Generally, the dominating group member is not a major problem for more than one or two sessions. The other group members tend to help the facilitators in controlling such a strong-willed parent, and often the dominating group member becomes aware of what he/she is doing and becomes less controlling or authoritative. It is also important for facilitators to remember that there will be natural shifts in the amount of participation; some parents will speak extensively one week but rather little the next week. Facilitators should not be too quick to become concerned with a highly verbal, strong-willed person. Remember, most of these parents are intense personalities.

THE WITHDRAWN GROUP MEMBER

It is important that the group facilitators note whether one of the group members seems shy and withdrawn. Facilitators can encourage participation, but without putting that person on the spot. There is no need to rush this person; most group members speak as they become more comfortable with the group and often are getting quite important information simply by listening. Some people, by temperament, are simply reserved. Even so, the facilitators can assist this person by glancing frequently in that direction with an inviting look and perhaps extending an open palm gesture. The facilitator thus gives the person the opportunity to participate, but is non-confrontational. (Note: We do *not* suggest that you call on the person by name.) Likewise, the facilitator might wish to make a special effort to speak to that person before or after the group about matters in general or about the content of the session, or one of the facilitators may wish to sit directly next to this person during the next session to provide non-verbal support.

Finally, it is important that the facilitator give close attention to the non-verbal behaviors of the quiet parent. Does the parent seem to be listening interestedly? Does the parent keep coming week after week? If so, that parent is likely benefitting from the group and will speak when he/she is ready.

THE INSIGHTLESS GROUP MEMBER

Sometimes parents engage repeatedly in behaviors which are not helpful to them, their family, or their interactions with the school with no seeming awareness that their behaviors are not helpful and may be a part of their problem. Despite several attempts by facilitators and various group members to help them understand, they continue to seem totally lacking in insight concerning what they are doing. It is important for the group facilitators to remember that you cannot bludgeon insight into others, and that probably this person is doing the best that he/she can at this time.

The insightless group members are often the most frustrating ones to group facilitators; patience is extremely important. Typically, the other group members will encourage the insightless group member to try some particular behavior and may even be gently confrontive to the parent. When the parent tries some different behavior, the facilitator (and the other group members) can "catch him doing something right." Insight, in this case, will usually come after the behavior change, not before it. Anticipatory praise can be very helpful in getting the insightless parent to try a different behavior or way of looking at matters.

THE HOSTILE GROUP MEMBER

Occasionally, a group member may give a seemingly unlimited string of "Yes, but...," will criticizingly pontificate to the other parents, or will describe—and endorse—an extremely angry pattern of interactions with his/her children. To meet such a person head on would likely cause an explosion and would not be very helpful. Instead, it is important to remember the motto of *Guiding the Gifted Child,* which is "flowing with rather than fighting against." When a group member is hostile in this fashion, it is usually helpful to react initially to the "Yes, but..." with silence or to find something good about what the person has done or said. It is important with hostile people to remember that, in the same way as "where there is smoke, there is fire," it is also true that "where there is anger, there is hurt, pain, or fear underneath." Thus, a gentle response of understanding or admiring may often defuse the situation and models a different way of interacting.

With the hostile group member and the dominating group member, the approach of an indirect interpretation may be particularly appropriate. An indirect interpretation is a statement that is made ostensibly to one parent but which really is directed at the parent who has spoken previously. For example, the hostile group member may have described a very angry interaction with his children. A few minutes later, a facilitator might say to another parent, "I really admire how you listened to your children. It really is so very important, isn't it, for parents to not let themselves get overly angry to the point that they have trouble listening to their children and thereby jeopardize their relationships with them." Such an indirect interpretation is usually not lost on the person who needs to hear it, but is an interpretation that is far less likely to arouse defensiveness or to put the person's ego on the line. Anticipatory praise can be important here also.

THE FRAGILE GROUP MEMBER

Sometimes, though rarely, a group member may be particularly emotionally sensitive or feeling overwhelmed by life situations and may become quite tearful or upset. When this occurs, the groups are almost always extremely supportive of that group member. Our experience indicates that this is most likely to occur in the topic on stress or depression, in which a parent may have a child who has attempted suicide or voiced thoughts of suicide, or in which one of the parents has known someone who is or has been quite depressed. On other occasions, the emotional upset may occur because the parent's ability to cope is temporarily overwhelmed by life's pressures.

One of the reasons we so strongly suggest that there be two (or perhaps three) facilitators is for this very reason. By glancing around the group, the facilitators are continually monitoring what is happening in the group, as well as "eye-checking" with each other. If one group member appears to be upset, one facilitator can give an imperceptible nod to the other facilitator, who will focus non-verbally on giving support to that parent. If the upset continues or seems extreme, one facilitator will then get up from his/her chair to walk quietly around behind the upset parent and whisper in that parent's ear, "Are you all right? Would you like to step out in the hall and talk a little bit there for right now?"

The facilitator and the parent leave the room and talk about whatever is happening with the parent. Usually, they return after only five or ten minutes, and the parent is now functioning quite well. The facilitator and the parent both take their seats without comment, and the returning facilitator gives a barely perceptible smile and a nod to the other facilitator. Unless the parent wishes to say something, nothing is said to the group. Our experience is that the group is comfortable with this process as long as the facilitators appear reasonably comfortable. Also, the parents will subsequently express a great deal of support in indirect ways to the parent who became upset.

Occasionally, there is a parent who simply has too many problems or too few coping abilities to profit from a support group such as this and who needs intense professional help. It is certainly acceptable for the group facilitator—either while talking before or after a group session—to suggest privately to that parent that perhaps professional assistance should be considered now, and to try the next parent group series rather than continuing to participate in the current series. This scenario, however, happens very rarely.

Instead, parents often get professional help while continuing to participate in the parent group series, and this seems to work quite well. Remember, though, these are *not* therapy groups.

CHAPTER IX

The Action Plan

"The longest part of the journey is said to be the passing of the gate."
–Marcus Terrenius Varro

"If you don't know where you're going, any road will do."
–Midwestern Proverb

We hope that the training sessions and this training manual will stimulate you to establish SENG model parent support groups in your locale and that you will do so promptly. In the same way that we say to parents about the groups, we want this training manual to have take-home value for you. The following outline is an expansion of the checklist in *Appendix A* and will help in many of the "nuts and bolts" issues that need to be considered in order to successfully establish these groups.

SETTING

PLACE

Where can you hold your meetings? What is the atmosphere, and what are the expectancies created by that location?

Churches and schools may not provide an atmosphere where parents feel free enough to discuss wide ranges of issues, though in some communities that is certainly not true. For example, in many African-American communities, churches are a preferred place to meet. Libraries often have meeting rooms that can be used (usually for free), and older children can study or quietly enjoy themselves in the library while their parents are meeting. Other possibilities might include civic centers, retirement homes, YMCA facilities, etc. It is important to consider whether a particular location is attractive to diverse cultural and socio-economic groups. African-American, Native American, Appalachian, or other cultural groups may find themselves feeling uncomfortable in some settings and may be reluctant to attend or participate fully.

Very practical matters, such as parking and room size, need to be considered as well. If you are meeting in the evening, is the parking lot well-lighted? Is there sufficient parking, or is the lot filled by people attending other meetings at the same location? Is it safe for parents to stand by their cars talking after the sessions? Is the parking lot sufficiently close that you will be able to carry your materials to the room without difficulty?

TIME

Some facilitators hold their group meetings in the evening; others during the day. Either seems fine, although the type of parent attending may vary depending on whether the sessions are in the morning or in the evening. Morning sessions, for example, tend to bring those who are not employed outside of the home, who are self-employed or have flexible working hours, or who work second or third shift.

We would emphasize that we have found that one and one-half hours seems to be an ideal length of time to cover the topics each week. Less time than this is insufficient for all group members to participate, and more than ninety minutes can be a burdensome commitment for many parents. The other most important aspects are that the group meeting times should be regular ones, and there should be time (ten to fifteen minutes) for the groups to run over should it not be possible to bring them to a close exactly on time. Additionally, there should be time for the co-leaders to talk before the group, as well as to process the happenings at the conclusion of each group session. Occasionally, one week's session may have to be postponed because it falls during a holiday week (e.g., Thanksgiving). This does not seem to be a problem. However, more than one postponed session can disrupt the flow of the group.

FEE SCHEDULE

Prior to establishing the groups, the facilitators need to agree on a fee schedule. We would encourage you not to let finances prevent parents from obtaining services (perhaps getting donations to underwrite some of the costs for parents who are financially strapped), but it is generally advisable to have parents pay at least some fee. People usually value things that they have to pay for more than they value things that they obtain for free. Some facilitators in private practice settings will charge approximately $150.00 for the ten session series (this includes two persons attending from each family). Other facilitators, particularly those from an agency or who are operating under a school's auspices, will charge only $30.00 for the ten session series, which is sufficient to cover the cost of the book, handouts, and if necessary, rental of a meeting space.

In establishing your fee schedule, you will need to consider that some parents will wish to come just for one session to see if it is appropriate for them. Other parents may already have a copy of *Guiding the Gifted Child*. The facilitators will need to decide what they will do in such circumstances. In general, we would recommend that you allow such flexibility, including allowing parents to join the group up to the third session. (If they cannot attend starting with the third session, then they should wait for the next series of SENG groups.)

You will also need to decide which of the facilitators (if either) will be paid, and if so, how much. To maintain rapport between facilitators, it is recommended that they agree to the same financial arrangements, either donating their time or receiving an equal amount of stipend.

ADVERTISING YOUR PROGRAM

It would be helpful for you to do some thinking about the parents you are trying to reach. Are they parents of gifted children in general? Are they parents from a particular segment of the community? Are you trying to reach parents from a particular school district or from a variety of school districts? Will you attempt to reach parents who are home-schooling their gifted children?

Once you have decided, you will, of course, want to make contacts with relevant school and community leaders and with other key persons, such as leaders in state or local gifted child associations and parents who are leaders in gifted advocacy groups. Although these persons may or may not refer parents to the group, it is important nonetheless that they know what you are planning to do and that your groups are not therapy or advocacy groups. Otherwise, you are likely to have opposition from some of these people, which can be a notable handicap to your program.

School personnel (e.g., coordinators of gifted programs, teachers of the gifted, etc.) should be informed quite early, as well as local, county and state associations for gifted and talented. Because schools play such an important part in children's lives, it is most important to seek the input and assistance from teachers and coordinators of gifted programs. Certainly, you don't want to alienate them! Parent support groups or advocacy groups for talented children should likewise be involved. It often is very helpful to inform mental health professionals (psychologists, psychiatrists, social workers, etc.) as well as social service agencies.

Depending on the extent of your contacts, you may be able to get a great deal of assistance in publicizing the availability of your groups. Often, these persons are quite willing to post flyers (e.g., on library bulletin boards), give you mailing lists, put an announcement on a local Internet web page, or help you publicize in other ways. Newspapers, particularly weekly papers, are typically delighted to run a small story on establishing the groups, on characteristics of these children, and on the needs of parents of talented children. Other possibilities to be considered include speeches to PTA/PTO groups, radio talk shows, or church groups.

PROFESSIONAL LIAISONS

It is very important to know a few psychologists, psychiatrists, pediatricians, mental health counselors, etc. to whom parents might be referred should there be a need for some specialized guidance or therapy services. For example, the parents may have a child who is both gifted and learning disabled or who is both gifted and attention deficit disordered. You may, however, have to slowly educate some of these professionals about talented and gifted children; unfortunately, few such professionals receive significant formal training in the area of able, bright, creative children. As mentioned earlier, we are not advocating that you run legal risks by recommending specific professionals. You can probably indicate the names of persons or agencies that you understand have worked with families of gifted children and encourage parents to inquire whether other parents have had helpful experiences with various professionals. Most facilitators feel comfortable in pointing out to parents what questions they might wish to consider when shopping for professional assistance and encourage parents to ask such questions of professionals whom they are considering visiting.

OTHER RESOURCES

Prior to establishing the groups, facilitators should become familiar with various educational and community alternatives for bright, high potential children. This information should not only include public school programs, but also private and parochial schools as alternatives. Preschool programs, Saturday enrichment programs, museums, universities with programs for bright children, Internet resources, summer camps, after-school community activities—all of these are handy resources to have available for the parents. In addition, it is very helpful to have available informational materials about local and state associations for parents and teachers of talented and gifted children as well as newsletters and publications. Teachers and coordinators of gifted and talented programs often have such information readily available.

Listings of local resources and associations can usually be obtained directly from coordinators of gifted programs, from the headquarters of the state associations for talented and gifted, from the state coordinator of gifted programs, or by searching the Internet. The National Association for Gifted Children (NAGC) can also provide helpful information. You may contact them at: NAGC, 1155 Fifteenth Street NW, Suite 1002, Washington, D.C. 20005. Telephone: (202) 785-4268.

ACQUIRING RESOURCE MATERIAL

Appendix A provides a checklist of materials you will want to acquire before beginning the SENG parent groups. Books for the lending library, as well as copies of *Guiding the Gifted Child,* can be acquired directly from the respective publishers. Titles of various books which have been very helpful for parents of gifted children are listed in *Appendix B: Books for Families with Gifted Children*. Sometimes publishers have "bruised" copies of books which they will sell at a significant discount if you ask. Names and addresses of several relevant publishers are listed at the end of *Appendix B*. Obtaining the books for the lending library usually takes about two to four weeks from the time you place your order.

Other resource materials are listed in the appendices to this training manual. *Appendix C* lists periodicals of interest. *Appendix D* provides addresses of several relevant national and international associations which focus on gifted children and their families. *Appendix E* lists Internet resources for parents and educators of gifted children. *Appendix F* provides guidelines for parents and teachers to promote more helpful interactions between home and school.

References

Dreikurs, R. and Soltz, V. (1964). *Children: The Challenge.* New York, NY: Penguin.

Finesinger, J. (1948). Psychiatric Interviewing. *American Journal of Psychiatry.* 105 (3).

Karnes, F. and Marquardt, R. (1991a). *Gifted Children and the Law: Mediation, Due Process, and Court Cases.* Scottsdale, AZ: Gifted Psychology Press (formerly Ohio Psychology Press).

Karnes, F. and Marquardt, R. (1991b). *Gifted Children and Legal Issues in Education: Stories of Hope.* Scottsdale, AZ: Gifted Psychology Press (formerly Ohio Psychology Press).

Webb, J., Meckstroth, E. and Tolan, S. (1982). *Guiding the Gifted Child: A Practical Source for Parents and Teachers.* Scottsdale, AZ: Gifted Psychology Press (formerly Ohio Psychology Press).

APPENDIX A
Planning Checklist for Parent Groups

FACILITATORS

- Need two persons.

- Knowledgeable about group process/gifted education.

- Ability to encourage.

- Group facilitating skills that enable them to lead by modeling, using non-verbal techniques.

- Compatible with or a complement to each other.

- Committed to a ten week program.

- Make financial arrangements clear.

LOCATION, DATES, TIME

- An atmosphere which creates appropriate expectations.
- Comfortable sized room.
- Convenient parking.
- Proximity to group you're trying to reach.
- Dates compatible with school calendar.
- Evening or morning time.
- Facilities available for one and one half hours with preparation and process time.

FINANCIAL ARRANGEMENTS

- Decide fee.
- Sliding scale or financial aid arrangement.
- Decide to whom the checks will be made payable and when.
- When and how much facilitators will be paid.
- Decide discount for parents who already have a copy of *Guiding the Gifted Child*.

PROMOTE THE PROGRAM

- Depending on who sponsors the group, determine the target audience.
- Decide whether promotion will be internal or if the community is welcome.
- Determine content and format of promotion.
- Decide whether to utilize mailing, newspaper and other media announcements, posters in libraries or on other community bulletin boards, school counselors or psychologists, local gifted/talented parent group newsletter, word of mouth.

ACQUIRE RESOURCE MATERIAL

- *Guiding the Gifted Child: A Practical Source for Parents and Teachers.*

- Order books: Gifted Psychology Press, Inc.
P.O. Box 5057
Scottsdale, AZ 85261
Phone/Fax: 602/368-7862
Web site: www.GiftedPsychologyPress.com

- Prepare handouts, Weekly Session Evaluations, homework sheets.

- Assemble lending library—books and periodicals.

- Acquire lists of local resources: community opportunities, summer school, summer camps, school gifted/talented personnel, psychologists or counselors available for referral, gifted/talented associations and conferences, Internet resources.

APPENDIX B
Books for Families with Gifted Children

Adderholdt-Elliott, Miriam (1986). *Perfectionism: What's Bad About Being Too Good?* Minneapolis, MN: Free Spirit Publishing Co.

> *Written for teenagers and adults who have crossed the fine line between healthy ambition and destructive perfectionism. Topics such as procrastination, under-achievement, family and peer relationships, etc. are discussed, along with trouble signs and tips on how to take control of your life.*

Alvino, James (1985). *Parents' Guide to Raising a Gifted Child.* Boston, MA: Little, Brown & Co.

> *Ways parents can determine giftedness and specific tips for supporting and supplementing schools' efforts in nurturing individual giftedness.*

American Association for Gifted Children (1984). *On Being Gifted.* New York, NY: Walker & Co.

> *Reflections of twenty gifted teenagers about themselves and their giftedness.*

Barrett, Susan (1985). *It's All In Your Head: A Guide to Understanding Your Brain and Boosting Your Brain Power*. Minneapolis, MN: Free Spirit Publishing Co.

A manual for children to help them explore the possibilities and capabilities of their brain, how they learn and remember, and a discussion of logic and creativity.

Benson, Peter, Galbraith, Judy, and Espeland, Pamela (1998). *What Kids Need to Succeed.* Minneapolis, MN: Free Spirit Publishing Co.

Based on a nation-wide survey by Search Institute, the authors have identified 40 assets and 700 ideas for home, school, community and congregations to help kids succeed.

Berger, Sandra L. (1998). *College Planning for Gifted Students, Second Edition, Revised.* Reston, VA: Council for Exceptional Children.

Designed to help understand the unique needs of gifted adolescents as they plan for college, choose a school, and understand the application process, with an appendix of college guides, contests and competitions.

Bireley, Marlene and Genshaft, Judy (1991). *Understanding the Gifted Adolescent.* New York, NY: Teachers College Press.

Deals with educational and psychological issues of gifted adolescents, including the topics of career decision-making, sexuality, eating/anxiety/stress disorders, as well as issues of cultural minority adolescents.

Bloom, Benjamin (1985). *Developing Talent in Young People.* New York, NY: Ballantine Books.

Discusses the process of talent development in areas of music and art, athletics, mathematics and science. Biographical descriptions provide information about family patterns that promote talent development. Specific strategies are offered for parents and teachers to support and guide exceptional ability.

Clark, Barbara (1997). *Growing Up Gifted, 5th Edition.* Saddle River, NJ: Merrill/Prentice Hall.

> *This comprehensive resource book is one of the most often used texts for training teachers of gifted students. It is filled with research and practical suggestions for the classroom and home.*

Colangelo, Nicholas and Davis, Gary A. (1997). *Handbook of Gifted Education, 2nd Edition.* Boston, MA: Allyn and Bacon.

> *Scholarly without being pedantic, this book has 31 chapters by eminent authors and represents the latest thinking on topics such as intelligence, ability grouping, counseling and handicapped gifted.*

Cox, June, Daniel, Neil, and Boston, Bruce (1985). *Educating Able Learners: Programs and Promising Practices.* Austin, TX: University of Texas Press.

> *Examines practices found to be successful in meeting the special learning needs of high ability students. This book is based on the most recent national study by the Richardson Foundation, combined with data from a survey of MacArthur Fellows.*

Delisle, James (1987). *Gifted Children Speak Out.* Minneapolis, MN: Free Spirit Publishing Co.

> *This sometimes funny and poignant book resulted from questionnaire responses of over 6,000 gifted children. Sections on such topics as getting along with friends, school and defining giftedness are accompanied by stimulating discussion guides and group activities.*

Dreikurs, Rudolf and Soltz, Vicki (1964). *Children: The Challenge.* New York, NY: Penguin.

> *An extremely practical book which describes how to avoid power struggles, as well as how to help youngsters develop self-respect and self-management skills. Emphasizes how to let natural and logical consequences occur.*

Erhlich, Virginia (1985). *Gifted Children: A Guide for Parents and Teachers.* Englewood Cliffs, NJ: Prentice-Hall.

> *Extensive practical suggestions support this excellent look at understanding and encouraging gifted children. Discusses many areas of concern for parents of gifted children at home and at school.*

Faber, Adele and Mazlish, Elaine (1980). *How to Talk So Kids Will Listen, and Listen So Kids Will Talk.* New York, NY: Avon Books.

> *A practical guidebook for parent and child communication with examples of effective listening and responding styles.*

Featherstone, Bonnie and Reilly, Jill (1990). *College Comes Sooner Than You Think! The Essential Planning Guide.* Scottsdale, AZ: Gifted Psychology Press (Formerly Ohio Psychology Press).

> *For students and parents to use together. Covers evaluation of the student's strengths, exploration of careers, organization of records, preparing a resume, campus visits, planning finances, preparing for tests and filling out applications. Includes a month-by-month planning calendar starting in 8th grade.*

Feldhusen, John (Ed.) (1985). *Toward Excellence in Gifted Education.* Denver, CO: Love Publishing Co.

> *A primer on gifted education that examines most major issues. An excellent guide for anyone interested in cooperating with schools to provide programs to meet the needs of gifted children.*

Feldman, David (1981). *Nature's Gambit: Child Prodigies and the Development of Human Potential.* New York, NY: Basic Books, Inc.

> *Through case histories of six prodigies in writing, music and mathematics, the realm of exceptionally gifted persons is explored.*

Galbraith, Judy (1984). *The Gifted Kids Survival Guide (For Ages 10 and Under)*. Minneapolis, MN: Free Spirit Publishing Co.

> *Written for use by younger gifted children to help them understand the six great gripes of gifted kids, smart ways to make and keep good friends, how to prevent the perfection infection, and how to get what you want from life by setting goals.*

Galbraith, Judy and Delisle, James (1996). *The Gifted Kids Survival Guide: A Teen Handbook*. Minneapolis, MN: Free Spirit Publishing Co.

> *Written for the older adolescent, this book contains much practical advice and perspective, such as understanding test scores, learning ways to deal with depression and loneliness and how to take charge of one's life.*

Grost, Audrey (1970). *Genius in Residence*. Englewood Cliffs, NJ: Prentice-Hall.

> *Though now out of print, this book can be obtained through libraries. Anyone wanting to understand exceptionally gifted children will find invaluable information through this story of one family trying to find balance for their brilliant son in a normal world.*

Hall, Eleanor and Skinner, Nancy (1980). *Somewhere to Turn: Strategies for Parents of the Gifted and Talented*. New York, NY: Teachers College Press.

> *Contains excellent specific strategies to guide parents from their child's earliest years. A comparative developmental checklist helps parents identify giftedness in their children up to age three. Enrichment resources are explored.*

Heacox, Diane (1991). *Up From Underachievement*. Minneapolis, MN: Free Spirit Publishing Co.

> *Characteristics and profiles of underachievers are listed. Specific action plan strategies are given for parents, teachers and students.*

Johnson, Nancy (1989). *The Faces of Gifted*. Dayton, OH: Pieces of Learning.

> *A collection of articles addressing who the gifted are, traits of gifted children with particular discussion of gifted pre-schoolers, gifted at risk for experiencing problems, parent advocacy, home schooling, left brain/right brain and creativity.*

Jones, Claudia (1988). *Parents Are Teachers, Too: Enriching Your Child's First Six Years*. Charlotte, VT: Williamson Publishing Co.

> *Specific activities, ideas and problem-solving techniques on how to encourage pre-school children. These creative suggestions promote enhanced school readiness.*

Jones, Claudia (1990). *Encouraging Your 6-12 Year Old*. Charlotte, VT: Williamson Publishing Co.

> *More specific activities, ideas and problem-solving techniques to encourage children and to keep alive their motivation. Many of these ideas can be used for enrichment activities at home or at school.*

Karnes, Frances A. and Marquardt, Ronald G. (1991). *Gifted Children and Legal Issues in Education: Parents' Stories of Hope*. Scottsdale, AZ: Gifted Psychology Press (formerly Ohio Psychology Press).

> *Moving reports by parents who describe their search for appropriate and high quality education, their struggles with educational and legal obstacles and their creative solutions. Contains important advocacy information and specific guidelines for bridging the gap between home and school.*

Karnes, Frances A. and Marquardt, Ronald G. (1991). *Gifted Children and the Law: Mediation, Due Process, and Court Cases*. Scottsdale, AZ: Gifted Psychology Press (formerly Ohio Psychology Press).

> *Court cases involving gifted children at school or in domestic situations are compiled and analyzed, along with information on how to obtain due process and conduct mediation efforts. Highly readable and practical.*

Kerr, Barbara (1997). *Smart Girls: A New Psychology of Girls, Women and Giftedness.* Scottsdale, AZ: Gifted Psychology Press (formerly Ohio Psychology Press).

> *Bright girls have different needs because they face unique challenges and often show different patterns. This book provides guidance for parents and teachers. Brief biographies of eminent women are inspiring and insight-producing.*

McCutcheon, R. (1998). *Get Off My Brain: A Survival Guide for Lazy Students (Revised Edition).* Minneapolis, MN: Free Spirit Publishing Co.

> *An unconventional guide including study tips, using computers and the Internet and other fun and creative ways to help the unmotivated student achieve.*

Miller, Alice (1981). *Prisoners of Childhood* (previously titled *Drama of the Gifted Child*). New York, NY: Basic Books.

> *Promotes insight into the gifted child's view of the world. Helps parents avoid conveying to their child that they are loved only when they accomplish what their parents want.*

Piirto, Jane (1998). *Understanding Those Who Create, 2nd Edition.* Scottsdale, AZ: Gifted Psychology Press (formerly Ohio Psychology Press).

> *Synthesizes theory, research and practice in very readable fashion for parents and teachers. Presents information on what creativity is, how it is measured, and how it can be enhanced. Integrates Dabrowski theory and Myer-Briggs information. Particularly intriguing are discussions of characteristic life patterns of certain types of creative people.*

Reilly, Jill (1992). *Mentorship: The Essential Guide for Schools and Business.* Scottsdale, AZ: Gifted Psychology Press (formerly Ohio Psychology Press).

> *Some students learn better in mentorship settings. This practical book describes how to set up a successful mentorship program. Topics include discovering when a student needs a mentor, which students profit from mentorship programs, how to find mentors, how to prepare the student and the mentor and ready-to-use evaluation forms.*

Rimm, Sylvia (1990). *How to Parent So Children Will Learn.* Watertown, WI: Apple Publishing Co.

> *Focuses on how to prevent underachievement. This book highlights many common family patterns that lead to school learning problems and gives precise advice on how to deal with these problems.*

Saunders, Jacqulyn and Espeland, Pamela (1991). *Bringing Out the Best: A Resource Guide for Parents of Young Gifted Children.* Minneapolis, MN: Free Spirit Publishing Co.

> *This updated source book contains useful information to help parents bring out the best in their bright, talented child. Creative activities are suggested, along with information on such topics as choosing the right school and characteristics of gifted children.*

Schmitz, Connie and Galbraith, Judy (1985). *Managing the Social and Emotional Needs of Gifted Children: A Teacher Survival Guide.* Minneapolis, MN: Free Spirit Publishing Co.

> *A companion to the* Gifted Kids Survival Guide, *it contains dozens of concrete strategies for teachers of gifted education. Contents include resolving conflicts at school and at home, managing stress and handling feelings of differentness.*

Shore, Bruce M., Cornell, Dewey G., Robinson, Ann and Ward, Virgil S. (1991). *Recommended Practices in Gifted Education: A Critical Analysis.* New York, NY: Teachers College Press.

> *These authors have identified 101 commonly recommended practices in gifted education. Each practice is carefully scrutinized as to whether research really supports or refutes it.*

Smutny, Joan, Veenkeer, Kathleen and Veenkeer, Stephen (1991). *Your Gifted Child: How to Recognize and Develop the Special Talents in Your Child from Birth to Age Seven.* New York, NY: Ballentine.

> *How to identify and nurture academic aptitude, artistic expression and problem-solving.*

Vail, Priscilla (1989). *Smart Kids with School Problems: Things to Know and Ways to Help.* New York, NY: Dutton.

> *Ways to find the roots of academic problems. Practical ways to address auditory learning, visual learning, motor function and maturation.*

Walker, Sally Y. (1991). *The Survival Guide for Parents of Gifted Kids.* Minneapolis, MN: Free Spirit Publishing Co.

> *A good introductory book for parents which provides perspectives on how gifted children view themselves and the world, some typical problems that may occur (along with some advice on how to handle them) and an overview of educational options, with tips on how to advocate for your child's education.*

Webb, James, Meckstroth, Elizabeth and Tolan, Stephanie S. (1982). *Guiding the Gifted Child: A Practical Source for Parents and Teachers.* Scottsdale, AZ: Gifted Psychology Press (formerly Ohio Psychology Press).

> *This award-winning book provides time-proven guidance about such frequent concerns as motivation, discipline, peer relations, sibling relations, communication of feelings, stress management and depression. Very readable and practical.*

PUBLISHERS

You may wish to directly contact publishers that regularly carry books for parents and families of gifted children and focus on social emotional needs. Some of these are:

- **Free Spirit Publishing Co.**
  400 1st Avenue N, #616
  Minneapolis, MN 55401
  Phone: (800) 735-7323

- **Gifted Psychology Press, Inc.**
  P.O. Box 5057
  Scottsdale, AZ 85261
  Phone: (602) 368-7862

- **Pieces of Learning**
  1610 Brooklynn Drive
  Beavercreek, OH 45432
  Phone: (800) 729-5137

- **Prufrock Press**
  P.O. Box 8813
  Waco, TX 76714
  Phone: (800) 998-2208

APPENDIX C
Periodicals

Advanced Development: A Journal on Adult Giftedness, 777 Pearl Street, Denver, CO 80203.

> *This is the first journal on adult giftedness and focuses on issues that continue into adulthood.*

Gifted Child Quarterly, 1707 L Street NW, Suite 550, Washington, DC 20036.

> *Published by the National Association for Gifted Children, this scholarly journal features articles on a variety of topics and provides information about programs and conferences.*

The Gifted Child Today, P.O. Box 8813, Waco, TX 76714-8813.

> *Formerly G/C/T, this bi-monthly journal emphasizes articles on identifying and educating creative and gifted children. Activity ideas and information are helpful to families.*

Journal for Education of the Gifted, 1920 Association Drive, Reston, VA 22091.

> *Published by the Association for the Gifted of the Council for Exceptional Children (CEC-TAG), this scholarly journal presents research for administrators, teachers and other professionals, as well as enlightened parents.*

Parenting for High Potential, National Association for Gifted Children, 1707 L Street, #550, Washington, DC 20036.

> *A quarterly publication, this journal emphasizes parents' concerns and contains articles, lists of resources, frequently asked questions and announcements of upcoming events.*

The Prufrock Journal, P.O. Box 8813, Waco, TX 76714-8813.

> *This journal, which focuses on gifted education at the secondary level, is primarily written for practicing teachers. It emphasizes successful programs at the junior high and high school levels.*

The Roeper Review, P.O. Box 329, Bloomfield Hills, MI 48013.

> *A scholarly journal which presents academic, philosophical, social and emotional issues about gifted children and provides an expert update on research, information and book reviews.*

Understanding Our Gifted, P.O. Box 18268, Boulder, CO 80308-8268.

> *Particularly oriented toward parents, this journal provides information on books, conferences and issues about gifted children, particularly those who are highly gifted.*

APPENDIX D
Other Resources

American Association for Gifted Children/Talent Identification Program
  Duke University TIP
  1121 West Main Street, Suite 100
  Durham, NC 27701
  Phone: (191) 683-1400
  http://www.jayi.com/tip

American Mensa, Ltd.
  201 Main Street, Suite 201
  Fort Worth, TX 76102-3115
  Phone: (817) 332-2600
  http://www.us.mensa.org

Association for Bright Children
  19 Sherwood Drive
  Kingston, Ontario, CANADA K7M 2E2
  Phone: (613) 544-9585
  http://www.fcbe.edu.on.ca/SEAC/abchome.html

The Council for Exceptional Children (CEC)/The Association for Gifted
    1920 Association Drive
    Reston, VA 22091-1589
    Phone: (800) 328-0272
    http://www.aspensys.com

Council of State Directors of Programs for the Gifted
    c/o Michael Hall
    Specialist, Office of Public Instruction
    Montana Department of Education
    P.O. Box 202501
    Helena, MT 59620
    Phone: (406) 444-4422
    http://www.netc.org/web_mod/gifted_ed/

ERIC Clearinghouse on Handicapped and Gifted Children
    1920 Association Drive
    Reston, VA 22091-1589
    Library Phone: (703)264-9474 • TDD Phone: (703)620-3660
    http://www.cec.sped.org/ericec.htm

National Association for Gifted Children (NAGC)
    1707 L Street NW, #550
    Washington, DC 20036
    Phone: (202) 785-4268
    http://www.nagc.org

National Resource Center for Gifted and Talented
    University of Connecticut
    362 Fairfield Road, U-7
    Storrs, CT 06269
    Phone: (203) 486-4826 • Fax: (203) 486-2900
    http://www.ucc.uconn.edu:80/~wwwgt

Parents of Gifted and Talented Learning-Disabled Children
    2420 Eccleston Street
    Silver Spring, MD 20902
    Phone: (301) 986-1422

Supporting Emotional Needs of Gifted (SENG)
    405 White Hall
    Box 5190
    Kent State University
    Kent, OH 44242
    Phone: (330) 672-4450 • Fax: (330) 672-2512

World Council for Gifted and Talented
    18401 Hiawatha Street
    Northridge, CA 91326
    Phone: (818) 368-7501

APPENDIX E

Internet Resources for Parents/Educators of Gifted Children

Academic Talent/UC Berkeley—
   http://www-atdp.berkeley.edu

American Association for Gifted Children (AAGC)—
   http://www.jayi.com.aagc

American Creativity Association—
   ACAoffice@aol.com

Applying for College—
   http://www.collegenet.com

Arizona State Center for Academic Precocity—
   http://www-cap.ed.asu.edu/

Association for Supervision and Curriculum Development (ASCD)—
   http://www.ascd.org

Bibliography for Parents—
http://www.ctd.nwu.edu/ctdnet/resources/parents/parent_bibl.html

Council for Exceptional Children, Gifted—
http://www.cec.sped.org/ericec.htm

Duke Talent Identification Program—
http://www.tip.duke.edu

Education Program for Gifted Youth, Stanford—
http:www.epgy.stanford.edu/epgy/

ERIC Clearinghouse for Exceptional Children—
http://www.aspensys.com/eric/index.html

ERIC Digests on Gifted—
gopher://ericir.syr.edu/11/Clearinghouses/16houses/ERIC_EC/Gifted

Gifted and Talented (TAG) Resources Home Page—
http://www.eskimo.com/~user/kids.html

Gifted Child Society—
http://www.gifted.org

Gifted Children Monthly—
http:www.gifted-children.com/

Gifted Development Center (Linda Silverman, Denver)—
http://www.gifteddevelopment.com

Gifted Education Press Quarterly—
http://www.cais.com/gep

Gifted Education and Homeschool Resource Page—
http://members.aol.com/discanner/index.html

Gifted Listservers you can sign up for—
http://www.ctd.nwu.edu/ctdnet/resources/listserv.html

Gifted Psychology Press, Inc.—
http://www.giftedpsychologypress.com

Gifted Resource Council Family Resources—
http://www.cybam.grc/other.htm

Glossary of Gifted Education—
  http://members.aol.com/svennord/ed/GiftedGlossary.htm

GT World! A Meeting Place for Families and Friends of the G & T—
  http://www.gtworld.org/

High IQ Societies—
  http://www.crosslink.net/~quantam/hiq.html

Hollingworth Center—
  http://www.midcoast.com/~holo/hollingworth.html

Hoagies Gifted Education Page—
  http://www.ocsc.com/hoagies/gift.htm

Homeschooling the Gifted—
  http://www/geocities.com/Heartland/9687/SIG.html

Imagine: Opportunities for Talented Youth—
  http://jhunix.hcf.jhu.edu/~setmentr/imagine.html

Institute for Academic Advancement of Youth (IAAY), Johns Hopkins—
  http://www.jhu.edu/~gifted

Intuitor Page—
  http://ww.cris.com/~Tkrogers/index.html

Iowa Sate, OPPTAG (Precollege Programs)—
  http://www.public.iastate.edu/~opptag_infohomepage.html

Jacob K. Javits Gifted and Talented Education Program—
  http://www.ed.gov/prog-info/Javits/

Mecklenburg Parents for the Advancement of Gifted Education
  http://www.charweb.org/organizations/page/pagehome.html

Mensa, American—
  http://www.us.mensa.org

Midwest Talent Search (Northwestern University)—
  http://ctdnet.acns.nwu.edu/

Multiple Intelligences Bookshelf (bibliography)—
  http://ww.newhorizons.org/bibmishelf.html

National Association for Gifted Children (NAGC)—
http://www.nagc.org

National Excellence Report (U.S. Government, 1993)—
http://www.ed.gov/pubs/DevTalent/

National Foundation for Gifted and Creative Children—
http://www.nfgcc.org

National Resource Center on Gifted and Talented (NRC/GT)—
http://www.ucc.uconn.edu/~wwwgt/nrcgt.html

New Horizons for Learning—
http://www.newhorizons.org

Northwestern University Center for Talent Development—
http://nuinfo.nwu.edu/ctd/

Nurturing Intellectually Gifted Children—
http://www.cris.com/~Tkrogers/learnp.html

Online Educational Resources—
http://www.caso.com

Open Space Communications (*Understanding Our Gifted*)—
http://www.openspacecomm.com

Pitsco's Launch to Gifted and Talented Resources—
http://www.pitsco.com/p/gft.html

Project Zero, Harvard Graduate School—
http://pzweb.harvard.edu

Prufrock Press (*Creative Kids Magazine, Gifted Child Today*)—
http//www.prufrock.com

Resources for Gifted Education—
http://www.missouri.edu/~c618867/lanna/index.html

Rhode Island Advisory Committee on Gifted and Talented Education—
http://www.ri.net/gifted_talented/rhode.html

Rocky Mountain Talent Search, University of Denver—
http://www.du.edu/education/ces/rmts.html

Roeper Review—
  http://www.roeper.org/html/roeper-review.html

State Resources for Gifted Education—
  http://www.cec.sped.org/fact/stateres.htm

Surfing the Net with Kids—
  http://www.surfnetkids.com/feldman

TAG Family Network—
  http://www.teleport.com/~rkaltwas/tag/

TAGFAM—Families of the Gifted and Talented—
  http://www.access.digex.net/~king/tagfam.html

YAHOO Resources for/about Gifted Youth K-12—
  http://www.yahoo.com/text/education/k_12/Gifted_Youth

What Works!—
  http://www.teleport.com/rkaltwas/tag/articles/works/html

Zephyr Press—
  http://www.zephyrpress.com

APPENDIX F

Bridging the Gap Between Home and School: Guidelines for Parents and Teachers

1. Recognize that home and school have different goals, tasks, situations and constraints. Schools focus primarily on academic preparation, secondarily on socialization. At home, the focus is primarily on socialization, secondarily on academics.

2. Both are very important in their long-term effects on gifted children, though of the two, homes may be more crucial. The ideal is for both to work together, to avoid conflicts, or to bridge gaps.

3. Misunderstandings, differences in expectations and disappointments can usually be avoided if parents become involved in the school functions early and continually. Parents, making yourself known to teachers, principals, guidance counselors, etc. early and frequently is important.

4. Parents should offer to help teachers, librarians, etc. in ways that benefit *all* children, not just "gifted" students. Avoid appearing elitist. Gifted children's educational needs are often different, but gifted children are not necessarily "better."

5. Support school efforts to plan for able children. Help to interest the PTA and the school administration/school board in the topic. Support study groups on gifted children and similar cooperative endeavors. Ask if parents can attend school in-service programs on gifted children.

6. Parents, make periodic gifts of books, articles, or tapes about gifted children to the teacher, principal, guidance counselor, or librarian.

7. Parents and teachers must not give the impression of pushing or exhibiting a child, but should continually strive to give the child whatever he or she needs to reach his or her potential.

8. Teachers most often fear or expect that parents of gifted children will be "unguided missiles" and critically demanding of special favors for their children. Parents most often fear or expect that teachers will not understand and will retaliate on their children. Rarely is either one true.

9. Teachers are increasingly more informed about gifted children and their special educational needs, but are also often hampered by the constraints of the educational system within which they work and by their responsibilities to the other children they teach. The search for solutions to school problems must start with the realities of the classroom, in the same way that solutions to home problems must start with the realities there.

10. If a problem seems to exist between home and school, first consider that what the child tells you is that child's perception. The problem may be with the perception rather than with the situation.

11. Parent-teacher consultations are strongly recommended. Not only do they allow sharing of information and avoidance of being manipulated by the child, but they also promote building of a focused alliance to stimulate the child's achievement and self-concept.

12. Define concretely for yourself what you hope to accomplish in the parent-teacher meeting(s), and begin to formulate a specific plan for achieving those goals.

13. Prior to your conference, evaluate what *new* information you have and consider how your information might differ from what the teacher or parent knows about the child. Seek to *share* observations and information.

14. How much of your information can the other use constructively? Will your information demonstrate a pattern, promote understanding, or evoke compassion? Or will it frighten the other, lead to unhelpful behavior, or disrupt the relationship with the child?

15. Express understanding of the other person's feelings and viewpoints in the situation. Attempt to engage the other as an ally rather than as an enemy. Be sensitive to the other possibly feeling invaded.

16. Avoid blaming. Recognize that most persons do not act out of malice, but rather they drift into problem situations through oversight, lack of information, or by attempting to handle too many responsibilities. Only rarely is there a teacher or parent who just doesn't care or who is actively malicious.

17. Avoid trying to bludgeon insight or your point of view into others. It does not work and only results in resentment and hardening of positions.

18. Initially, ask for the other's overall perceptions of the child—how the child is doing and what the teacher's or parent's plans are. This allows you to learn where you are starting from and may bring some pleasant surprises.

19. Parents, give teachers professional respect in your approach, even if you must disagree at times. Teachers need support also. It is important that you not appear to be attacking the teacher's ability or character.

20. Teachers, parents need to feel genuinely listened to and respected, rather than like intruders or insignificant figures in the lives of their children. They are only seeking what is best for their children from their points of view.

21. In your conversations, avoid saying, "What are *you* going to do about... ?" Instead say, "What can *we* do about... ?"

22. In sharing new information, start with those parts most likely to fit with the other's perceptions and which will tend to build a common base from which to begin. Actively seek the other's opinions. Ask what the other thinks about each new piece of information.

23. Gradually share more information as the conversation progresses. Avoid dumping all of your complaints or new and different information onto the other. Instead, after each major piece of information, check to see how this fits with the other's perceptions or beliefs about the child or the situation.

24. Receive new information from the other as openly as possible, and ask questions in a spirit of curiosity rather than defensiveness.

25. When making a point, give examples and data rather than just general opinions.

26. If you have data from an outside expert, remember that this can often be quite threatening, since it tends to imply that the other is wrong. Try to present such information in ways that allow the other to not lose face.

27. Focus on solutions or attempts at problem-solving that are in small steps, measurable in outcome and achievable. Avoid broad, sweeping generalities, such as "improve self-concept."

28. Always attempt to give an alternative when making suggestions or recommendations.

29. Emphasize ways which show that working jointly is clearly preferable, and that it will make teaching or parenting easier or more enjoyable.

30. Try to come to agreement on some specific joint action plan, even if it represents only a partial solution, or to meet again.

31. If agreement is not reached or is only partially reached, do not insist on a definitive answer right then. Give the other person time to think and reflect on the new possibilities or new data.

32. Follow-up the conference with a brief letter of appreciation confirming your understanding of the issues, information and actions that are planned by each.

33. It may be wise to involve the guidance counselor, principal, or others in parent-teacher conferences, though this can leave one or more people feeling as though they have been ganged-up on. Realize that administrators must be supportive of their teachers, at least in public, but that they are typically also quite sensitive to concerns by parents and other members of the public.

34. Sometimes conferences do not work. Know when to give up trying to build a bridge or to change a situation. Instead, the focus may have to be on coaching the child to cope, building a safety net, or moving the child to a new class or new school.

35. Most of all, keep on modeling active problem-solving for the child!

APPENDIX G

About the Authors

JAMES T. WEBB, PH.D., ABPP-CL • CLINICAL PSYCHOLOGIST • P.O. BOX 5057 • SCOTTSDALE, AZ 85261

James T. Webb, Ph.D. is a clinical psychologist who is a frequent consultant and workshop speaker. Dr. Webb was the founder and Director of the SENG (Supporting Emotional Needs of Gifted) program in Dayton, OH. At that time, he was Professor and former Associate Dean for Special Programs at the School of Professional Psychology of Wright State University in Dayton, Ohio. Previously, Dr. Webb served as Director of the Department of Psychology at the Children's Medical Center in Dayton and as an Associate Clinical Professor in the Departments of Pediatrics and Psychiatry at the Wright State University School of Medicine. He has served on the Board of Directors of the National Association for Gifted Children and is a Past-President of the American Association for Gifted Children.

Dr. Webb was President of the Ohio Psychological Association and a member of its Board of Trustees for seven years. He was a member of the graduate faculty in psychology at Ohio University in Athens, Ohio from 1970 to 1975, where he taught psychological testing, community mental health, psychology and the law, and psychological research. He has been in private practice, as well as Chief Consulting Psychologist at the Western District Guidance Clinic in Parkersburg, West Virginia. Earlier, Dr. Webb was Program Coordinator for the Roche Psychiatric Service Institute in Nutley, New Jersey (1968-1970).

Dr. Webb has authored over 50 professional publications, including seven books, and presented numerous research and professional papers at state, regional and national psychology conventions. He is a frequent keynote speaker and workshop leader at conferences about gifted and talented children. Licensed as a psychologist, he is board certified as a Diplomate in Clinical Psychology. A fellow of the American Psychological Association, he served for three years as a member of its governing body, the Council of Representatives. Dr. Webb is also a fellow of the Society of Pediatric Psychology and the Society for Personality Assessment.

Dr. Webb is one of the authors of a pioneering and award-winning book which is entitled *Guiding the Gifted Child: A Practical Source for Parents and Teachers* (Scottsdale, AZ: Gifted Psychology Press—formerly Ohio Psychology Press). This book received excellent reviews in numerous publications including *Teaching Exceptional Children*, *Redbook*, and *The Wall Street Journal*. In 1983, this book won the National Media Award of the American Psychological Association as the Best Book for "significantly contributing to the understanding of the unique, sensitive, emotional needs of exceptional children." Born in Memphis, Tennessee, Dr. Webb completed college at Rhodes College and received his doctorate degree from the University of Alabama. He is the father of three daughters.

ARLENE R. DEVRIES, M.S.E. • DES MOINES PUBLIC SCHOOLS 1800 GRAND AVENUE • DES MOINES, IA 50309-3399

Arlene DeVries has held the position of Community Resource Consultant in Gifted and Talented Education for the Des Moines Public Schools since 1981. She has a masters degree in guidance and counseling and her special interest is the social and emotional needs of gifted students and their parents.

Mrs. DeVries received training from Dr. James Webb in the Supporting Emotional Needs of Gifted (SENG) program. Since 1985, she has conducted more than 50 ten week series of guided discussion groups for parents of gifted. She has teamed with Dr. Webb in conducting workshops throughout the country in training professionals to use the SENG model. A frequent speaker to parents of gifted children, she presents at numerous state and national gifted education conferences. She has presented the SENG guided discussion group model for parents of gifted children at World Gifted Conferences in The Hague, Toronto, Seattle, and in Hong Kong. Mrs. DeVries has served on the editorial board of *Roeper Review* and *Parenting for High Potential*, has many published articles in gifted education journals and was for many years chair of the Parent/Community Division for the National Association for Gifted Children. Prior to her current position as President of the Iowa Talented and Gifted Association, Mrs. DeVries served that organization as local parent chapter liaison.

Mrs. DeVries is active in Delta Kappa Gamma and Phi Delta Kappa education organizations and Sigma Alpha Iota professional music fraternity. She has taught music, kindergarten through high school, and currently teaches a popular adult education class entitled, "Learning to Enjoy Classical Music." She also presents a pre-concert preview of the music performed by the Des Moines Symphony one hour prior to each of its concerts.

As the parent of two talented children, she enjoys sharing with other parents ways in which they can help meet the special needs of talented and gifted children.

Index